Osama bin Laden

Titles in the FRONT-PAGE LIVES series include:

Osama bin Laden by Sean Price

Benazir Bhutto by Sean Price

Bill and Melinda Gates by Sally Isaacs

Nelson Mandela by Patrick Catel

Barack Obama by Michael Burgan

FRONT-PAGE LIVES

Osama bin Laden

Sean Stewart Price

Heinemann Library
Chicago, IL

www.heinemannraintree.com
Visit our website to find out more information about Heinemann-Raintree books.

To order:
☎ Phone 888-454-2279
▭ Visit www.heinemannraintree.com to browse our catalog and order online.

©2010 Heinemann Library
an imprint of Capstone Global Library, LLC
Chicago, Illinois

Edited by Adam Miller, Andrew Farrow, and Adrian Vilgiano
Designed by Kimberly R. Miracle and Betsy Wernert
Original illustrations © Capstone Global Library, LLC
Illustrated by Mapping Specialists
Picture research by Ruth Blair
Originated by Capstone Global Library
Printed and Bound in the United States by Corporate Graphics

15 14 13 12 11
10 9 8 7 6 5 4 3 2 1

ISBN 978-1-4329-6025-4 (sc)
ISBN 978-1-4329-3221-3 (hc)

Library of Congress Cataloging-in-Publication Data

Cataloging-in-Publication data is available at the Library of Congress

062011
006154

Acknowledgments

The author and publishers are grateful to the following for permission to reproduce copyright material: Corbis/Ahmad Yusni/epa **p.84**; Corbis/Bettmann **p.8**; Corbis/Bettmann **p.16**; Corbis/Brooks Kraft/Sygma **p.65**; Corbis/epa **p.69**; Corbis/Francis Dean/Sygma **p.63**; Corbis/Peter Turnley **p.53**; Corbis/Reuters **p.78**; Corbis/Sean Adair/Reuters **p.7**; Corbis/Sion Touhig **p.85**; Corbis/SYGMA **p.89**; Corbis/Vienna Report Agency **p.43**; Corbis/Wally McNamee **p.32**; Getty Images/Hulton Archive **p.25**; PA Photos/AP **p.72**; Rex Features **p.77**; Rex Features/Sipa Press **p.22**; Rex Features/Sipa Press **p.28**; Rex Features/Sipa Press **p.37**; Rex Features/Sipa Press **p.39**; Rex Features/Sipa Press **p.45**; Rex Features/Sipa Press **p.93**; Shutterstock background images and design features throughout.

Cover photograph of Osama bin Laden reproduced with permission of Getty Images/AFP.

We would like to thank Mark A. Berkson for his invaluable help in the preparation of this book.

Every effort has been made to contact copyright holders of any material reproduced in this book. Any omissions will be rectified in subsequent printings if notice is given to the publisher.

All the Internet addresses (URLs) given in this book were valid at the time of going to press. However, due to the dynamic nature of the Internet, some addresses may have changed, or sites may have changed or ceased to exist since publication. While the author and Publishers regret any inconvenience this may cause readers, no responsibility for any such changes can be accepted by either the author or the Publishers.

Table of Contents

Some words are shown in bold, **like this**. You can find out what they mean by looking in the glossary.

A Day in September

At 8:47 a.m. on September 11, 2001, a terrific boom rolled like thunder through the streets of New York City. Many people in the downtown area paused on their way to work to see what had happened. Those who looked up could see black smoke billowing from high up in the World Trade Center's north tower.[1]

Even among New York City's forest of skyscrapers, the World Trade Center stood out. The World Trade Center's Twin Towers were the fifth and sixth-tallest buildings in the world. On a typical day, at least 50,000 people worked in them. Another 140,000 people visited.[2] This was not a typical day, however. American Airlines Flight 11, carrying 75,710 liters (20,000 gallons) of jet fuel, crashed into the north tower. The explosion ripped through floors 90 to 100.[3]

NOT AN ACCIDENT

Television news channels began beaming images of the smoking tower around the world. Reporters tried to guess what had happened. Had the pilot made some terrible error? Was this an accident? Or was it something more sinister?[4]

The answer came at 9:02 a.m. Another jetliner appeared over the New York City skyline, coming in from the south. United Airlines Flight 175 skimmed over the tops of other buildings. Then, with an enormous fireball, the plane crashed into the south tower. Floors 78 through 87 blew apart.[5]

The north tower is seen here producing a pillar of black smoke as a raging fire burns away inside the building. The fireball (seen coming from the south tower) erupted when the second plane struck.

The truth was clear. Neither of these events had been accidental. The United States was under attack. And the attack was not over yet. On everyone's lips was the question, "Who could have done this?" News reports soon provided an answer: Osama bin Laden.

WHO WOULD DO SUCH A THING?

Osama bin Laden, a billionaire's son from Saudi Arabia, had launched terrorist attacks around the world before. But none of them compared to this onslaught. He turned September 11, 2001, into one of the bloodiest days in U.S. history. More than 2,900 people were killed.[6]

Who is Osama bin Laden? How did he go from being a respected citizen of Saudi Arabia to the most feared terrorist in the world? How did his **devout Muslim** beliefs lead him to see the United States as an enemy? How could his terrorist network—called al Qaeda—be stopped? And how could bin Laden himself be caught or killed? People the world over have been asking those questions since September 11.

Bin Laden's views are hateful to Americans. Most of the world's 1.2 billion Muslims also condemn his use of terrorism.[7] However, some Muslims see bin Laden as a hero. They hope to carry on his work. Understanding bin Laden—and what drives him—is the best way to understand why the September 11 attacks happened. It also helps us to understand why people join al Qaeda and support him in other ways.

Bin Laden's story begins in Saudi Arabia in 1957. . . . ❖

Headlines From 1957–1967

Here are some major news stories from the years of Osama bin Laden's childhood.

Soviet Dog "Laika" Becomes First Earthling in Space

The **Soviet Union** put the first live being into space on November 3, 1957. It was a little dog named Laika. Just a month before, the Soviets launched *Sputnik 1*. This was a satellite—the first human-made object to go into space. The *Sputnik 1* launch started a "space race" with the United States. These rival countries rushed to build their space programs.

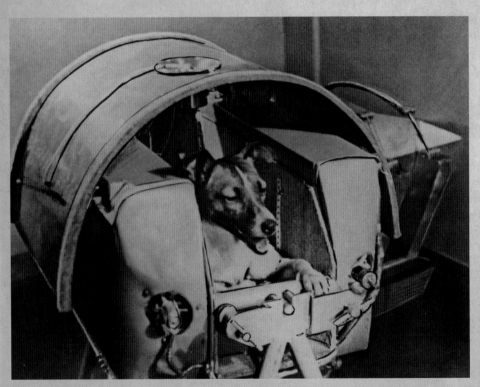

Laika the dog blasted into Earth orbit aboard the Sputnik 2. She had been a stray, wandering the streets when scientists found her. This led Americans to nickname her "Muttnik." She was trained only briefly before being put aboard the metal carrier which fit inside Sputnik 2. Unfortunately, there was no plan to bring Sputnik 2 back to Earth, and Laika died in space after only a few hours.

Rev. King Makes "I Have a Dream" Speech

On August 28, 1963, in Washington, D.C., more than 200,000 peaceful demonstrators heard the civil rights campaigner Reverend Martin Luther King, Jr., make one of the most powerful speeches in U.S. history. King said that he dreamed of a day when whites and blacks would live together in peace and harmony.

President Kennedy Assassinated

U.S. President John F. Kennedy was shot by an assassin in Dallas, Texas, on November 22, 1963. The youthful Kennedy's death was a shock to many around the world. Kennedy was shot by a troubled former U.S. marine named Lee Harvey Oswald. Oswald himself was shot while in police custody by a man named Jack Ruby.

Mao Zedong Launches Cultural Revolution

Chinese **communist** leader Mao Zedong launched the "Cultural Revolution" in 1966. The Cultural Revolution was an effort to rid the country of anti-communist influences. But Mao also used it to destroy his opponents within the Communist party. Millions of people were killed or imprisoned.

Star Trek Airs for First Time

The science fiction television show *Star Trek* was shown for the first time in 1966. The show only stayed on the air for three years. But it became one of the most popular shows of all time in reruns. *Star Trek* led to a series of popular movies as well as other spin-off television shows.

Growing Up bin Laden

*The mastermind behind the September 11 attacks grew up in one of the world's most extraordinary families. Osama bin Laden was born in 1957 in Riyadh, the capital city of Saudi Arabia (see map). His exact birthday is unknown. Many believe it is March 10.[1] He was named after a companion to the Prophet Muhammad, the founder of **Islam**. Osama's name means "the lion."[2]*

Osama's mother, Alia, was a Syrian-born woman. She was one of about 22 women married to Osama's father, Muhammad bin Laden. Like almost everyone in Saudi Arabia, Muhammad was a Muslim, or follower of Islam. Under Islamic law, a man is permitted four wives—if he can care for them equally. Even so, it is extremely rare for any Muslim man to have more than one wife. But Osama's father was a rare man. Osama was the 17th of his father's 54 children.[3]

Osama's family was not unusual for its size alone. His father was a self-made man—a billionaire who started life as a penniless worker. Muhammad bin Laden was born in 1908 and grew up in a poverty-stricken part of Yemen called Hadhramawt. It is a collection of mud-brick towers so ancient that it is mentioned in the Bible's book of Genesis. In the 1920s, Muhammad left Yemen for neighboring Saudi Arabia. He had nothing except a sharp mind, a strong personality, and an ability to work very hard.[4]

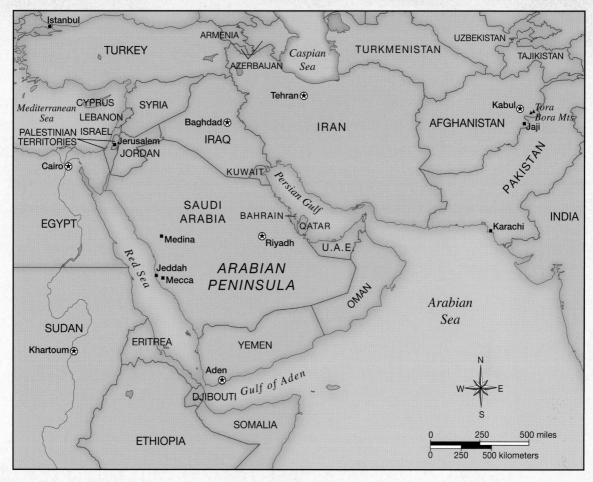

Osama bin Laden was born in Riyadh, Saudi Arabia in the Middle East, but his eventful life took him to many areas around the region, including Sudan and Afghanistan.

BUILDING AN EMPIRE

Muhammad labored first as a dockworker in the port city of Jeddah, Saudi Arabia. Later, he worked as a bricklayer.[5] But he was lucky. Oil was discovered in Saudi Arabia in 1938. Before then, some people lived in cities, but much of the area was populated by desert nomads, people who herded animals like sheep and goats and traveled by camel, horseback, or on foot. These tribespeople followed an especially strict version of Islam called **Wahhabism**. It rejected almost all modern conveniences and inventions like electricity, plumbing, radios, or cars.

The discovery of oil in the kingdom changed all that. By the 1950s, the Saudi royal family found itself awash in billions of dollars generated by oil sales. Over the protests of many traditionalists, they began to modernize the country. Saudis were suddenly building schools, water plants, **mosques** (Muslim houses of worship), and mansions for the family of King Abdul Aziz. In the early 1950s, Muhammad bin Laden started his own construction business. He gained a reputation as an honest and reliable builder.[6]

A BIG OPPORTUNITY

Muhammad soon won important contracts to build new palaces for the Saudi royal family. The king liked Muhammad so much that he named him an honorary minister of public works. At the time, Saudi Arabia had very few good, paved roads. So Muhammad began building roads. In fact, his company—Saudi Binladen Group—built almost all the roads in the Saudi kingdom. This work made Muhammad rich. But he continued to live modestly. "Our house was of a lower standard than most of the houses of the people working for us," Osama later remembered.[7]

OSAMA BIN LADEN'S EARLY YEARS

Osama spent his early years in his father's house. He was just one of a crowd of children by various wives. Getting attention from such a busy, important father was next to impossible. On Islamic feast days, Muhammad would kiss each child and give him or her a coin. One time Osama recited a poem to his father and was rewarded with 100 **riyals** (the Saudi form of money), a large sum. Sometimes Muhammad would gather his children into his office to see how his family was growing. Otherwise, Osama had little to do with his father.[8]

Muhammad divorced Osama's mother when their only child was about four or five. Osama's father liked to marry his ex-wives off to important friends and employees. In this case, Osama's mother married one of Muhammad's executives, a man named Mohammed al-Attas. Together, they would have three boys and a girl. Al-Attas was a good stepfather to Osama. In many ways Osama acted as a third parent in the family with his younger half-siblings.[9]

Osama's mother remembered him as "a shy kid, very nice, very considerate. He has been always helpful. I tried to instill in him the fear and love of God, the respect and love for his family, neighbors and teachers."[10]

Young Osama enjoyed television. He especially liked westerns like the U.S. television show *Bonanza*. Osama also loved riding horses. So it was natural that he enjoyed the U.S. television show *Fury*. It was a story about a boy and his black stallion. The martial arts movies of Chinese actor Bruce Lee appealed to his love for action and adventure.[11]

"He has been always helpful. I tried to instill in him the fear and love of God, the respect and love for his family, neighbors and teachers."
—Osama bin Laden's mother, talking about him

But entertainment options were limited for everyone who lived in Jeddah in the 1960s. There were no theaters, malls, museums, or other distractions. Jeddah was still a poor port town surrounded by blazing desert. A woman named Carmen Dufour later married one of Osama's half-brothers. In her book, *Inside the Kingdom: My Life in Saudi Arabia*, she described the main part of Jeddah at that time. "Donkey Square was a crisscross of dirt tracks where people came to buy water from men leading donkeys with barrels on their backs," she wrote. "There were no parks, no flowers, not even trees. This was a place without color."[12]

> *"There were no parks, no flowers, not even trees. This was a place without color."*
> —Carmen bin Laden

THE DEATH OF MUHAMMAD BIN LADEN

Most Saudi citizens were not allowed to fly private planes. That was reserved for the royal family and the military. Muhammad bin Laden was an exception. He needed to fly constantly to each of his far-flung projects. But on September 2, 1967, Muhammad's private jet plane crashed, killing him. He had been on his way to marry yet another bride.[13]

The death of Muhammad bin Laden was big news in the Middle East. He was considered a Saudi national hero for paving roads in dangerous areas that nobody believed could be paved. In fact, he had built most of the modern structures in Saudi Arabia.

Muhammad had so many children that several of them met for the first time at his funeral. Muhammad's death was a terrible blow to 10-year-old Osama. Like all his brothers, he would always feel that he was living in this great man's shadow.[14] ❖

Mecca and Medina

Muhammad bin Laden was a deeply religious man. His proudest achievements were his projects in the Saudi cities of Mecca and Medina (see map on page 11). Mecca is the birthplace of the prophet Muhammad and it is the home to the Grand Mosque, the holiest house of worship for Muslims. All Muslims pray in the direction of Mecca wherever they are in the world, and a visit to Mecca is one of the Five Pillars of Islam (obligations for all Muslims who are able). Medina is the home to the Prophet's Mosque, the second-holiest. All Muslims are expected to visit this one, as well.

In the 1940s and 1950s, the mosques were crumbling from neglect and overuse. So the government hired Muhammad bin Laden to expand and modernize the facilities. It was delicate work that took decades to complete. Muhammad often brought in his sons to watch. They saw worn-out old buildings torn down and new concrete ones replace them. It is not clear how much of it Osama witnessed. But he later showed an intimate knowledge of the work.[15]

Muhammad also later did work on the Al-Aqsa mosque in Jerusalem (which was then part of Jordan), Islam's third-holiest site. Good Muslims are expected to pray five times a day. Osama liked to brag that his father—thanks to his private airplane—could pray in Mecca, Medina, and Jerusalem all in the same day.[16]

HEADLINES FROM 1968–1978

Here are some major news stories from the years bin Laden was forming his conservative beliefs.

The Czechs' Prague Spring Does Not Last

In 1968 the communist country of Czechoslovakia, in eastern Europe, launched a series of **reforms**. These reforms were designed to give people more freedom to speak, read, and travel. This period was called the "Prague Spring." (Prague was Czechoslovakia's capital.) However, Czechoslovakia was part of the Warsaw Pact. That was a group of countries loyal to the Soviet Union. The Soviets invaded Czechoslovakia and put an end to the reforms. Many Czechs bravely protested against the Soviet invasion, at the risk of being killed or imprisoned.

Armstrong Becomes First Person to Walk on the Moon

On July 20, 1969, U.S. astronaut Neil Armstrong became the first person to walk on the Moon. Armstrong's landing capped an effort started in 1961 by U.S. President John F. Kennedy to send an astronaut to the lunar surface.

Anti-War Protestors Shot at Kent State

Four students at Ohio's Kent State University were shot and killed by national guardsmen on May 4, 1970, during an anti-war protest. The protestors were rallying against the U.S. invasion of Cambodia. That invasion was carried out to help with the U.S. war in Vietnam. Anti-war protests swept college campuses nationwide. The shootings further divided public opinion about the war.

Kent State students disperse as the National Guard fire tear gas. Two men and two women were killed and others were injured when soldiers fired on a crowd of about 500 students.

Pong Becomes First Popular Video Game

First released in November 1972, Pong became the first widely popular video game. Pong was simply a computerized, two-dimensional version of ping-pong. It had very simple graphics and was easy to use. It is credited with causing the later explosion in popularity of video games.

Israel Fights Yom Kippur War

A **coalition** of **Arab** nations, led by Egypt and Syria, launched a surprise attack against Israel on October 6, 1973. (See page 23 for more on the history of conflict in the region.) The invasion came on Yom Kippur, a Jewish holiday. The Arab countries did well in the first 48 hours. However, momentum soon swung to the Israelis. The war ended on October 26, with neither side winning a clear victory.

Oil Embargo Causes Price Shocks in the United States

Gasoline prices soared in 1973 after Arab oil-producing countries refused to ship oil to the United States. Saudi Arabia and other oil-rich countries said that they were punishing the United States for its support of Israel. The oil cutoff caused widespread shortages of gasoline for the first time. The soaring cost of gasoline suddenly pumped billions of dollars into Saudi Arabia's economy.

Religious Awakening

As a teenager, Osama bin Laden was an average student in school. However, he attended al-Thagr, which was one of the toughest, most prestigious schools in Saudi Arabia. The students there did not wear the traditional Saudi dress of a thobe *(a long, flowing robe) and a headdress. Instead, they followed the example of British prep schools. Each student wore a jacket, tie, pants, and shirt.[1]*

A schoolmate remembered bin Laden:

> [He was] an honorable student. He kept to himself, but he was honest. If you brought a sandwich to school, people would often steal it as a joke and eat it for themselves if you left it on your desk. This was a common thing. We used to leave our valuables with Osama because he never cheated. He was sober, serious. He didn't cheat or copy from others, but he didn't hide his paper, either, if others wanted to look over his shoulder.[2]

WAHHABI ISLAM

Saudi Arabia is a very religiously conservative country. The Wahhabist Islam that is taught there teaches a strictly literal interpretation of the **Qu'ran**, the holy book of Muslims. (It is also known as the Koran.) Anything not mentioned in the Qu'ran is suspect. For instance, Muslim **clerics** in Saudi Arabia at first opposed the use of telephones. They grudgingly accepted them only after they listened to people recite

*"He kept to himself, but he was honest. . . . .
He was sober, serious. He didn't cheat or
copy from others, but he didn't hide his paper,
either, if others wanted to look over his shoulder."*
—A former classmate, describing
Osama bin Laden as a schoolboy

verses from the Qu'ran over the phone. Followers of Wahhabist Islam also believe that all other people—even other Muslims who are not Wahhabists—are condemned to hell.[3]

In eighth grade, the sober, serious bin Laden had what friends described as a religious awakening. It was helped along by his gym teacher. The teacher was a member of a group called the Muslim Brotherhood. Many in the Brotherhood believed that all governments in the Middle East should follow a **radical** form of Islam.[4] Bin Laden became a devoted member of a group of students who met with the teacher. He joined the Brotherhood as well, and his behavior became more religious.

Bin Laden refused to listen to music produced by instruments (which many conservative Muslims see as un-Islamic).[5] He also stopped watching his favorite television shows and ditched his pants and tie for Saudi clothes after school was out. "You know how kids joke," bin Laden's friend Batarfi recalled. "[But in bin Laden's presence] we watch our words, don't use bad words because it's like having a priest around. You watch your mouth and your behavior."[6]

LOVING ADVENTURE

Bin Laden was more religious than most people his age. But he was not boring to be around. He loved playing soccer. He also enjoyed poetry and music, as long as there were no instruments involved. His family owned what they called a "farm"—although it was really a patch of desert. There he was able to ride horses and race around in jeeps. He loved to ride or drive fast over sand dunes, even though he often crashed dangerously while doing so. He also liked to shoot guns from horseback, just like a cowboy. His family vacations included mountain climbing in Turkey and big-game hunting in Kenya.[7]

A STRICT MARRIAGE

In 1974, while he was still in high school, bin Laden married for the first time. Just 17 years old, he married a 14-year-old cousin named Najwa Ghanem. She was the daughter of his mother's brother and came from his mother's village in Syria. Like bin Laden, Najwa was tall, somewhat gangly, and attractive. In the years that followed, she would be almost constantly pregnant. They would have 11 children together.[8]

Like a typical Saudi wife, Najwa obeyed bin Laden on all matters. Carmen bin Laden recalls that one time Osama and Najwa's infant son Abdullah needed water. Bin Laden insisted that the boy drink from a spoon. He refused to let Najwa use a rubber bottle nipple because, apparently, he believed it violated the Qu'ran. But the baby would not drink from the spoon. So it suffered and cried for hours. Najwa did not dare defy bin Laden. "A wife in Saudi Arabia cannot do anything without her husband's permission," Carmen bin Laden later wrote. "She cannot go out, she cannot study, often cannot even eat at his table. Women in Saudi Arabia must live in obedience, in isolation, and in the fear that they may be cast out and summarily divorced."[9]

A DOTING FATHER

But unlike his own father, bin Laden doted on his children. He loved to laugh and play with both sons and daughters. He especially liked to take them to the beach (though they had to dress modestly, even in the water). He also liked to take them camping in the desert. If it was cold, they would cover themselves with sand for warmth. They also learned how to handle both horses and camels. Bin Laden refused to let his children go to school. Instead he paid for tutors. He wanted to control every aspect of his children's upbringing. "He wanted to make them tough, not like other children," one of bin Laden's friends said.[10]

THE FAMILY BUSINESS

By 1976 bin Laden had enrolled in college. Most of his brothers went overseas to Europe or the United States to get degrees. They attended some of the world's best universities, including Oxford and Harvard. But bin Laden stayed in Saudi Arabia and attended King Abdul Aziz University in Jeddah. It was a new college with just a few hundred students. Bin Laden studied economics. However, his head was not in his textbooks. He was more interested in trying to win a place in the bin Laden organization, which was now run by his older half-brothers.[11]

"I want to be like my father...
I will work day and night with no rest."
—Osama bin Laden

Bin Laden's brothers finally gave him a job working near Mecca in 1978. Each day after class he would race to Mecca. His task was to level hills to make room for new hotels and roads that the bin Ladens were building. The job was expected to take six months. Bin Laden vowed to do it even more quickly. "I want to be like my father," he said. "I will work day and night with no rest." Like his father, bin Laden worked side-by-side with ordinary laborers. However, this brutally hard schedule took its toll. Bin Laden soon dropped out of college, one year short of graduation.[12]

As it turned out, the year 1979 was one of upheaval in the Muslim world. The events of that year would help send bin Laden in a new, more radical direction. ❖

In 1967, tensions between Israel and the surrounding Arab countries were quickly escalating. Arab states had never accepted Israel's creation as a country in 1947, and had made many threats to attack. Egypt made the first recognizable act of war, by blocking Israel's southern port. Israel launched a successful attack against Egypt in response, then beat back attacks from Jordan and Syria, gaining land from both countries as a result. The tensions that caused the Six-Day War, and others that resulted from it, still exist today.

Israel and the Muslim world

For hundreds of years, Muslims and Jews lived in relative tolerance. But since the 1920s, politics in the Middle East have revolved around disputes between these two religious groups.

In 1948 the "Jewish state" of Israel was carved out of lands that had belonged to Palestinians since Roman times. Palestinians are **Arabs** who are mostly Muslims. So other Muslim countries—including Saudi Arabia—sided with the Palestinians in trying to take their land back.[13] The Jews had occupied the land thousands of years before, until they were expelled by the Romans in 70 C.E. So many Jews believe that they are entitled to the land. This disagreement over the land is the heart of the Israeli/Palestinian conflict.

Since 1948 Israelis have fought off several serious attacks by neighboring countries. In 1967 the Israelis succeeded against these attacks during a conflict called the Six-Day War. Israel also won new territory, including the city of Jerusalem. Jerusalem is a city that is holy to Muslims and Jews (as well as Christians).

Jerusalem's fall to Israel was a huge blow to Muslim pride. Many young Muslims tried to join the war to retake Jerusalem. Muhammad bin Laden made a serious attempt to convert his company's bulldozers into tanks to fight Israel. A teacher at Osama bin Laden's school said many of the boys there "wanted to get on buses to go and join the good cause [of fighting Israel]." The school had to convince them that getting an education was the best way to fight back.[14]

Jerusalem's fall was one of many factors that helped to turn many Muslims toward a more radical version of their beliefs. After 1967 Muslims throughout the Middle East began to question their governments. They believed that their leaders' lack of religious belief had caused the losses to Israel. They argued that all Muslims should follow Islamic laws more closely.

HEADLINES FROM 1979

Here are some major news stories from the year of the invasion of Afghanistan.

Camp David Talks Bring Peace

In 1979 Egypt's President Anwar Sadat made history by signing a peace treaty with Israel. The two countries had fought off and on since Israel was founded in 1948. The agreement gave hope for a wider peace between Israel, a mostly Jewish country, and its Muslim neighbors. Egypt and Israel held their peace talks at Camp David, a wooded presidential retreat in Maryland. U.S. President Jimmy Carter hosted the peace talks.

Nuclear Accident Causes Scare in Pennsylvania

The Three Mile Island nuclear power plant near Middletown, Pennsylvania, released radioactive steam into the air on March 28, 1979. The steam was released when a water pump broke down. The accident was caused by a combination of human error and equipment failure. Many feared that the plant's 500 workers could have become contaminated. Critics said the accident showed that nuclear power plants are not safe.

Bhutto Executed in Pakistan

On April 4, 1979, former Pakistani Prime Minister Zulfikar Ali Bhutto was hanged, despite widespread appeals to save his life. Bhutto was hanged on orders of the man who overthrew his government a year before, General Zia ul-Haq. Bhutto was one of Pakistan's few democratically elected leaders. Zia replaced Bhutto's rule with a military **dictatorship** that strictly followed Islamic laws.

Thatcher Becomes First Woman Prime Minister of Great Britain

On May 4, 1979, Margaret Thatcher became Great Britain's first female prime minister, the nation's highest-ranking elected official. Thatcher's Conservative, or Tory, party won a large majority in Parliament. Thatcher's strong personality would win her the nickname the "Iron Lady."

Margaret Thatcher shortly after becoming Prime Minister. She is the second person from the left.

Sony Introduces the Walkman

The Sony Corporation began selling the first Walkman portable cassette tape players on July 1, 1979. The Walkman became the first of many portable music systems. Before the Walkman, people had to carry around large, clumsy tape players or small tape players that had poor sound quality.

A Year of Radical Change

Three dramatic events occurred in 1979 that shook the Muslim world. These events increased radicalism in the Muslim world. They also had a profound effect on Osama bin Laden and his family in Saudi Arabia.

They were:
- *The overthrow of the shah (king) of Iran*
- *The invasion of Mecca's Grand Mosque by Muslim radicals*
- *The Soviet Union's invasion of Afghanistan.*

For bin Laden, who was then 21 years old, the first two of these events shaped his life profoundly, though indirectly.[1] But the invasion of Afghanistan became very personal. It turned him first into a national hero. Later, it made him into the world's most wanted terrorist.

THE FALL OF THE SHAH OF IRAN

The shah of Iran was overthrown on January 16, 1979. Mohammad Reza Shah Pahlavi had ruled Iran since September of 1941, when he replaced his father Reza Shah, who had ruled before him. He had made Iran into an ally of the West, and had tried to modernize the country. He was backed by the United States. But he had also stolen billions of his country's oil wealth. He had arrested or killed anyone suspected of speaking out against him.[2]

But the government that replaced that shah was even more ruthless. Iran was soon led by a Muslim cleric, Ayatollah Ruhollah Khomeini. Khomeini imposed harsh new rules based on radical Islam. Women were stripped of most of their rights. Those who wore makeup or foreign clothing often had acid thrown in their faces. Meanwhile, most western music, movies, and television shows were strictly forbidden. In 1979 a group of students, who were later backed by Khomeini, seized the U.S. **embassy** in Tehran, the capital. They held the Americans as hostages for 444 days.[3]

"Everyone in the Middle East
could feel the sudden,
sinister wind of change"
—Carmen bin Laden

A TIME OF EXTREME CHANGES

Until the Iranian revolution, several Middle Eastern nations—including Saudi Arabia—had been moving toward greater openness. But the Saudi ruling family feared that a Khomeini-like figure might overthrow them as well. To seem stricter, the Saudi leaders had the religious police, or *mutawa*, crack down hard on un-Islamic or Western behaviors, many of which were forbidden. For example, children's dolls were banned because human images are forbidden by the Qu'ran. Stereos were smashed. Possession of whisky would lead to being jailed and beaten.[4]

Even before 1979, all women in Saudi Arabia wore a *burqa* or *abaaya*. This is a large cape that hangs over the head and covers the body. It is usually combined with a veil over the face. By wearing the *abaaya* and veil, every part of a woman is covered except her hands and feet (though there is an opening for the eyes).[5] After the Iranian revolution, women like bin Laden's wife, Najwa, began wearing gloves, despite the searing desert heat. The religious police might beat a woman if any skin showed.[6]

Other Muslim countries saw similar crackdowns, though usually not as severe. "Everyone in the Middle East could feel the sudden, sinister wind of change" caused by the Iranian revolution, wrote bin Laden's sister-in-law Carmen bin Laden.[7]

These Iranian demonstrators are showing their support for the Ayatollah Khomeini and the fall of the Shah.

INVASION OF MECCA'S GRAND MOSQUE BY MUSLIM RADICALS

On November 20, about 500 radicals led by Juhaiman Al-Otaibi seized control of Mecca's Grand Mosque, the holiest place in Islam. They also took dozens, perhaps hundreds, of innocent worshipers as hostages. This revolt caught the Saudi ruling family completely off guard. The Saudi police and military found that the rebels were almost impossible to attack. The renovations done by Muhammad bin Laden (see page 15) had unintentionally turned the mosque into a fortress.[8]

The mosque's giant loudspeakers normally called people to prayer. Now they were used to broadcast the rebels' complaints about the Saudi government. They wanted Saudi Arabia to become radically isolated. They said it should reject all things modern. It should also break off relations with the United States and Europe and stop selling oil to them. They saw these non-Islamic cultures as deeply immoral.

A person could be executed in Saudi Arabia for even hinting at opposition to the royal family. But the rebels called for removing the king and creating a new, more Islamic government.[9]

A DIFFICULT QUESTION

Crown Prince Fahd, who then headed the Saudi government, faced a dilemma. People respected the royal family in large part because it was the caretaker of Islam's two holiest mosques. If Fahd waited to starve out the rebels, people might see him as weak. The rebels and their demands might gain support. Saudi Arabia might see a revolution like the one that had just rocked Iran. But if Fahd launched an attack, he would be unleashing bloodshed and violence in the holiest of all Muslim places. This would clearly violate the Qu'ran, which says that not even a plant may be uprooted within the Grand Mosque.[10]

But Fahd received clerical approval and so opted for an attack. After two bloody weeks, the last group of 63 rebels surrendered. About 200 people died before the rebels surrendered, including hostages, rebels, Saudi police, and soldiers. The captured rebels were soon beheaded in Saudi Arabia's largest mass execution. During the fighting, bin Laden's older brothers helped the government forces. The bin Ladens were the only ones who had detailed maps of the Grand Mosque's many rooms and chambers.[11]

Bin Laden himself was briefly arrested, though. The police mistook him for being a rebel sympathizer. At the time, bin Laden really was a strong supporter of the royal family. But the rebel attack helped change his mind. Later he would say that Crown Prince Fahd defiled the sanctity of the Grand Mosque—meaning he had made its holiness impure. Bin Laden also came to agree with the terrorists' demands. Like them, he would favor a more isolated Saudi Arabia and the overthrow of the royal family.[12]

THE SOVIET UNION'S INVASION OF AFGHANISTAN

On Christmas Eve 1979, Soviet tanks rolled into the poor neighboring country of Afghanistan (see map on page 11). For Muslims around the world, this was the greatest shock in a shocking year. The Soviet Union was a union of communist republics that required its subjects to be atheists (people who do not believe in God). It was unthinkable for devout Muslims to allow a whole country of Islamic brothers and sisters to be forced into atheism.[13]

According to one of bin Laden's closest friends, bin Laden had never even heard of Afghanistan up to that point. Nevertheless, the news that fellow Muslims were being attacked and killed demanded his attention. News quickly spread that thousands of **refugees** were fleeing Afghanistan, pouring into neighboring Pakistan. Most of them were caught in refugee camps, where they had little food, water, or shelter. "I was enraged and went there at once," bin Laden later claimed. "I arrived within days, before the end of 1979."[14]

Bin Laden's involvement in Afghanistan began almost as a hobby. But it became an obsession. Osama bin Laden would soon help lead a holy war against the Soviets in Afghanistan. ❖

Sayyid Qutb: The godfather of Al Qaeda

Killing is a terrible sin in Islam. According to the Qu'ran, killing one innocent person is as bad as killing "all mankind."[15] The sayings of the Prophet Mohammed expand on this idea. They say that a Muslim cannot kill another Muslim except under certain severe circumstances. Those who kill on other occasions can expect eternal punishment.[16]

So how do Muslims like those who took over the Grand Mosque or those intent on killing Soviets—or like terrorist groups such as al Qaeda—justify killing innocent people and other Muslims? The answer can be found largely in the writings of Sayyid Qutb, a member of the Muslim Brotherhood. Few people in the United States or Europe have heard of him. Yet he is a very influential writer in the Muslim world.

After spending some time in the United States, Qutb was disturbed by the materialism and other qualities of life in a free country. He hated it and those like it in western Europe. He believed these countries gave people too much personal liberty. That allowed them to become immoral. Qutb saw this as a battle between God and Satan. There was no middle ground. Qutb believed the only proper government is an Islamic **theocracy**—a government in which religious leaders rule in the name of God. This put him at odds with the Egyptian government, which executed him at age 59 in 1966. But Qutb's teachings spread widely after his death.[17]

After the September 11, 2001, attacks, the United States formed a commission to investigate what had happened. The commission's report would outline Qutb's influence on bin Laden.[18]

HEADLINES FROM 1980–1987

Here are some major news stories from the years of Afghanistan's war with the Soviets.

Reagan Elected President

Former movie star and California governor Ronald Reagan was elected U.S. president in November 1980. Reagan came into office promising a more conservative government. He wanted to cut taxes and reduce the role of government in people's lives.

Prince Charles Marries Lady Di

Prince Charles, the heir to the British throne, married Lady Diana Spencer in what was widely described as a "fairy tale" wedding. Millions of people worldwide watched the July 29, 1981 ceremony on television.

July 29, 1981. The newly married Prince Charles and Princess Diana stand with Queen Elizabeth II on a balcony of Buckingham Palace.

Suicide Bomber Kills 241 Marines in Lebanon

On October 23, 1983, a suicide bomber driving a truck full of explosives leveled the U.S. Marine barracks in Lebanon (see map on page 11). The explosion killed 241 people. The Marines were in Lebanon as part of an international peacekeeping operation. It was the single deadliest day for the marines since World War II. The bombing caused the United States to abruptly pull its forces out of Lebanon.

Personal Computers Become Popular

The spread of personal computers began in the mid-1970s. But the introduction of newer, faster computers in the early 1980s caused an explosion in personal computer sales. Many of these computers were made by Apple, which introduced the first Macintosh computers on January 24, 1984. The "Mac" was the first computer to use a "mouse."

Gorbachev Becomes Soviet Leader

On March 11, 1985, Mikhail Gorbachev was named supreme leader of the Soviet Union. Gorbachev's rise to power marked a serious change for the world's leading communist country. Gorbachev called for greater freedom of expression for individuals. He also called for greater economic freedom. These changes would later lead to the collapse of the Soviet Union in 1991.

The Wreck of the Titanic Found

Seventy-three years after it sank, a joint U.S.–French team discovered the wreck of the *Titanic*. Some boasted that the giant passenger ship was unsinkable. However, it hit an iceberg on its first voyage. The ship sank tragically on April 15, 1912, killing 1,595 people. The discovery of its wreck on September 4, 1985, helped shed new light on the disaster.

The *Mujahideen*

As 1980 dawned, Osama bin Laden appeared to be a lucky man. He was rising steadily in the bin Laden organization.[1]

He also took more wives. As a young man in college, bin Laden vowed to follow the Prophet Mohammed's example and have four wives. This was unusual, because having multiple wives had become socially unacceptable in Saudi Arabia. But he wanted to show that having multiple wives worked.[2] Bin Laden married his second, third, and fourth wives in the early 1980s. In time, these women would bear him 19 children. (Later, in 2000, he would marry a 17-year-old Yemeni girl named Amal, after one of his wives divorced him. Little is known about her except that she later gave birth to a girl.)

FIGHTING THE SOVIETS

More and more, bin Laden became caught up in the Afghan fight against the Soviets. Bin Laden mostly worked as a fundraiser for the Afghans at first. His work was an extension of the Saudi government's efforts. As Muslims, the Saudis naturally opposed the Soviet invasion. They secretly looked for ways to undermine the Soviets' **occupation** of Afghanistan.

At the same time, the United States was fighting the **Cold War** against the Soviets. The Cold War was a mostly nonviolent conflict between the two countries that had begun in 1946. Americans were also eager to weaken the Soviet occupation.

Both the United States and Saudi Arabia began secretly giving millions of dollars to the Afghan fighters. Neither country could risk doing this in the open. It might trigger war with the Soviet Union. So they gave the money to a third country, Pakistan. Pakistan is also a Muslim country, and it shares a long border with Afghanistan (see map on page 11). Pakistan's government secretly bought weapons and supplies and gave them to the Afghan fighters.[3]

"I used to hand over the money and head straight back, so I wasn't really familiar with what was going on [on the battlefield]."
—Osama bin Laden

Private individuals also gave money to the Afghan cause. Much of that money was used to help war refugees. However, a lot of it went to the **mujahideen**. That was the Arabic word for the Afghan fighters. *Mujahideen* is related to the word *jihad* and is understood to mean "holy warriors." Between 1980 and 1983, bin Laden shuttled back and forth between Saudi Arabia and Pakistan a lot. With the private encouragement of the Saudi government, he raised money for the *mujahideen* among wealthy Saudis. Then he took the money to *mujahideen* groups and their supporters in Pakistan.[4]

"I used to hand over the money and head straight back, so I wasn't really familiar with what was going on [on the battlefield]," bin Laden later said.[5]

HOLY WAR

Like most other Muslims, bin Laden saw the fight against the Soviets as a *jihad*. This word is often understood to mean simply "holy war on behalf of Islam." However, it has a deeper meaning to Muslims. It more often refers to doing one's utmost in a personal struggle. Usually it is a struggle to become a better Muslim.[6]

Saudis admired what bin Laden was doing. The king himself approved of it (though he could not say so openly). Bin Laden was no longer just Muhammad bin Laden's 17th son. He had become an important man in the bin Laden family.[7]

THE FIRST BATTLE

At first, bin Laden did not join the fighting. His mother had forbidden him to go near it. The Saudi government also told him to stay away. He was too important. Bin Laden listened to them. But in June 1984, he crossed over into Afghanistan for the first time. He went to a mountain camp in an area called Jaji. It was near a Soviet outpost.

"I asked forgiveness of God Almighty…"
—Osama bin Laden

"I asked forgiveness of God Almighty, feeling that I had sinned because I listened to those who advised me not to go [earlier]," he later said. "I felt that this four-year delay could not be pardoned unless I became a **martyr** [for Islam]." A martyr is someone who endures suffering or death for a cause.[8]

The first battle bin Laden saw came on June 26, 1984. At 7 a.m. Soviet jets screamed in to attack the sleeping camp at Jaji. Bin Laden was shocked that the explosions from the Soviet missiles drowned out the booming of the Afghan cannons. He marveled that the Afghans shot down three Soviet jets without a single loss. But he was embarrassed as well. The **Arabs** in the camp, like himself, had dived for trenches the minute the fighting started. The more experienced Afghans had stood their ground and fought.[9]

Osama bin Laden is shown here in a cave in Afghanistan, during his involvement in the Afghan-Russian war.

ABDULLAH AZZAM

More and more, bin Laden became tied to Abdullah Azzam. Azzam was a lively, well-liked Palestinian religious scholar and teacher. He was already famous when he became prayer leader at King Abdul Aziz University, bin Laden's school. According to the award-winning foreign relations journalist Lawrence Wright, Azzam "mesmerized audiences with his vision of an Islam that would dominate the world through force of arms." Like bin Laden, he felt called to participate in the Afghan fight as a way of defending Islam.[10]

Bin Laden and Azzam found that they made a good team. Azzam was passionate and outgoing—a natural recruiter for Muslims who wanted to fight against the Soviets. However, Azzam did not have much money.

Meanwhile, bin Laden was still a shy, quiet man who seldom impressed people upon a first meeting. However, he possessed a personal fortune, and he could raise even more.[11]

Though bin Laden was rich, he led a very basic lifestyle. This was also part of his personal *jihad*. He wanted to become tougher and to make his children tougher. Azzam marveled that even in Jeddah's blazing heat, bin Laden seldom turned on his air conditioner unless guests were there. "He lives in his house the life of the poor," Azzam reported. "I never did see a single table or chair. Any Jordanian or Egyptian laborer's house was better than the house of bin Laden. At the same time, if you asked him for a million riyals [Saudi money] for the *mujahideen*, he would write you out a check on the spot."[12]

RECRUITING FOR WAR

In 1984 Azzam and bin Laden agreed to boost Arab involvement in the war. Azzam issued a *fatwa*, an opinion on religious law by an Islamic scholar. His *fatwa* declared that fighting *jihad* in Afghanistan was the duty of every able-bodied Muslim. This *fatwa* was endorsed by Saudi Arabia's chief cleric. At the same time, bin Laden made a tempting offer. He promised a plane ticket, a residence, and living expenses for every Arab—and the person's family—who joined in the fight. This was a lot of money for any poor Muslim living in the Middle East.[13]

LOVE OF MARTYRDOM

Many Muslims, including some women, went to Pakistan so that they could fight. Most of the volunteers who came had something in common—they wanted to become martyrs. Being a martyr promised many rewards in paradise, the afterlife they hoped to enjoy. Poor martyrs were told that they would be given unbelievable riches in the afterlife. At one Afghan camp, the Arab fighters pitched their white tents in an exposed place. The tents were easy targets for Soviet bombers. "We want them to bomb us," one Arab fighter told a reporter. "We want to die!"[14]

This picture from 1989 shows Soviet fuel tankers on fire due to an Afghan ambush near the end of the war.

But the Afghans did not really want Arabs as fighters. Rather, they wanted Arab money to buy weapons. So most of the Arab recruits ended up doing relief work with the millions of Afghan refugees who fled to Pakistan and other nearby countries. (By the war's end in 1988, there were 3.27 million Afghan refugees overall.)[15] And when at first bin Laden did try to take his men into battle, it ended in failure. His men panicked under pressure or arrived too late when needed.

THE "LION'S DEN"

Bin Laden's chance to make his mark as a fighter finally came in 1987. He and his men suffered through a bitterly cold winter in the mountains around Jaji.[16] Friends tried to warn bin Laden that his position was a death trap. But he refused to listen. He called the position "the Lion's Den." He used the bin Laden family's bulldozers to build trenches and caves to make it easier to defend.[17]

> *"After the battle of Jaji, he was looked upon as a military man who deserved to be a leader."*
> —An Egyptian filmmaker, describing Osama bin Laden after the battle of Jaji in Afghanistan

---

A series of battles broke out around Jaji in April. Though the Arab fighters were badly trained and inexperienced, they fought ferociously. The Soviets were driven back. "I saw [bin Laden] with my own eyes on the battlefield," said an Egyptian filmmaker who was present. "He was in the middle of the fighting. Being a rich man, no matter what he was like, people of course looked at him as a financier, just a man with money. After the battle of Jaji, he was looked upon as a military man who deserved to be a leader."[18]

The victory at Jaji gave bin Laden and his men confidence as warriors. However, the fighting had no impact on the outcome of the war. The Afghans had already nearly forced the Soviets from the country. The war was winding down. The Soviets would begin leaving Afghanistan in 1988, with all troops fully withdrawn by February 15, 1989.[19] ❖

Bin Laden and the CIA

Since the September 11, 2001, attacks, many people have claimed that Osama bin Laden received financial aid and training from the U.S. **Central Intelligence Agency (CIA)** during the Afghan war against the Soviets. The CIA is the United States' top overseas spy agency. It poured about $3 billion into the war.[20]

However, there is no evidence that bin Laden—or any other Arabs—received any CIA money or training. The CIA had little reason to help bin Laden. The real fighting in the war was done by Afghans, not Arabs. Bin Laden's efforts were a sideshow. Also, bin Laden was already getting help from Saudi intelligence agencies. He did not need the CIA's help.[21]

Even if the CIA had offered money or assistance, it is unlikely that bin Laden would have accepted. Bin Laden bitterly disliked the United States. He would not even drink soft drinks such as Coke or Sprite because they were made in the United States.[22]

However, the United States does bear some responsibility for bin Laden's rise to power. The United States, Saudi Arabia, and Pakistan all applauded the influx of Arab fighters to Afghanistan. These fighters would later become the core of bin Laden's army. All three countries would later endure terrorist attacks from these men.[23]

Also, bin Laden did receive accidental help from the CIA and the U.S. military. In the early 1990s, an Egyptian-American man named Ali Mohamed joined bin Laden's cause. Mohamed was a U.S. Army sergeant. He may also have worked with the CIA, though that is disputed.

There is no doubt, though, that Mohamed gave bin Laden U.S. Army manuals showing how to make bombs out of household chemicals, like aspirin. He also showed bin Laden's men how to be more effective terrorists. He trained them in planting bombs, assassinating foreign leaders, and hijacking planes. In fact, he personally trained bin Laden as well as other top al Qaeda leaders. Mohamed was finally arrested by the U.S. government in 1998.[24]

HEADLINES FROM 1988–1991

Here are some major news stories from the years bin Laden spent forming al Qaeda.

Protestors Killed in China's Tiananmen Square

For seven weeks in 1989, pro-democracy protestors took over Tiananmen Square in the heart of Beijing, China. They called for greater openness in China's communist government. But on June 4, the government sent in soldiers who killed hundreds of people and arrested thousands more.

The Berlin Wall Falls

On November 9, 1989, Germans celebrated the fall of the Berlin Wall, one of the most hated instruments of communist rule in eastern Europe. Since 1961 the wall had separated free West Germany from communist East Germany. The wall's collapse meant that millions of people in eastern Europe were free to visit other parts of the world for the first time. It also showed that the Soviet empire was crumbling.

Failed Takeover Leads to the Collapse of the Soviet Union

On August 19, 1991, Soviet leader Mikhail Gorbachev was overthrown by several of his top advisors. The leaders wanted to stop many of Gorbachev's reforms. They expected popular sympathy. Instead, the public rallied behind Russian President Boris Yeltsin. After three days, the takeover ended. That quickly led to the collapse of the Soviet Union.

Prehistoric Man Found in Glacier

In September 1991, two German tourists discovered the remains of a 5,300-year-old man in the Alps near the border of Austria and Italy. He was the oldest natural mummy ever found in Europe. The mummy helped show scientists many things about how prehistoric people lived.

There were also several items found near the mummy, who became known as Ötzi, including a bow with arrows, a dagger, an axe, and a wooden backpack.

From Hero to Outcast

The Saudi press turned Osama bin Laden into a national hero after the defeat of the Soviets. News reports in Saudi Arabia made it sound as if he and his Arab fighters had toppled the Soviet Union single-handedly. After 1988 people began calling bin Laden "Sheik Osama." The title sheik *is a sign of respect. It is usually given to a religious leader or the head of a large group or family.*[1]

Arab recruits now poured into Pakistan. They were looking for a chance to join the anti-Soviet *jihad*. Few would get a chance to fight in Afghanistan. But bin Laden still saw them as valuable recruits. He had spent a lot of time and money building a small army. Osama ran his camps just like any military camp that gives basic training. Recruits had to be physically fit, and the camps trained them to be good soldiers. He felt it would be a shame to see that army disband now. He already had a bigger war in mind—a war to preserve and protect Islam worldwide.[2]

AN INTERNATIONAL ORGANIZATION

By 1988 bin Laden surrounded himself with more and more radical men. Most of them were from Egypt. These men had spent terrible years being tortured in Egypt's prisons for opposing the government there. They had become **fanatical** about toppling Egypt's leaders. They also wanted to tear down other Arab governments that they considered un-Islamic. They were considered religious radicals. These are people who believe in a

AL-ZAWAHIRI   BIN LADEN

This image clearly shows Ayman al-Zawahiri and Osama bin Laden recording a statement.

strict version of Islam based on a literal interpretation of the Qu'ran and other related writings.

Ayman al-Zawahiri was the leader of these Egyptian radicals. He was a medical doctor who first met bin Laden in 1986. By 1988 he had become bin Laden's trusted counselor. Many have argued that he controlled bin Laden. At one point, a close friend of bin Laden's tried to visit. He was told bin Laden was unavailable because "Dr. Ayman was giving him a class in how to become the leader of an international organization."[3]

This "international organization" would become the terrorist network al Qaeda. The idea for al Qaeda, which means "the base" in Arabic, was officially developed in August 1988. The name *al Qaeda* came about almost accidentally. The training camps for the group were originally called al Qaeda Al-Askariya, or "the Military Base." But the name *al Qaeda* also had the meaning of a base, as in a foundation—something to build on.[4]

> ## *"We have to make a stand against America because it helps Israel."*
> ## —Osama bin Laden, 1990

A JOB WITH BENEFITS

Historian Lawrence Wright says that bin Laden ran his new group, al Qaeda, just like a business:

> New recruits filled out forms in triplicate [three of each form], signed their oath of loyalty to bin Laden, and swore themselves to secrecy. In return, single members earned about $1,000 a month salary; married members received $1,500. These would be good salaries for anyone in the Middle East. In addition, everyone got a round-trip ticket home each year and a month vacation. There was a health-care plan and for those who changed their mind—a buyout option: They received $2,400 and went on their way.[5]

Ironically, one of al Qaeda's first targets may have been Abdullah Azzam, bin Laden's old friend (see page 37). Azzam had become far more **moderate** than bin Laden. He had wanted to fight Israel, not carry on a *jihad* against the United States or other Arab governments. On November 24, 1989, he was killed by a car bomb in Pakistan. His murder was never solved. It is unlikely that bin Laden had anything to do with his death. But Zawahiri remains one of several top suspects. He hated Azzam's moderate views and may have feared Azzam would get in the way of working with bin Laden.[6]

LEAVING AFGHANISTAN

Once the Soviets left Afghanistan in 1989, the country slid into **civil war**. The different *mujahideen* factions that had fought so bravely against the Soviets now turned on one another. Bin Laden sided with the radical Muslim commander Gulbuddin Hekmatyar. Before long, bin Laden and other Arabs were pressured by other Afghan commanders—and the Pakistanis—to go back home.

But many of the Arab fighters could not return home. Their governments did not want them. Unlike bin Laden, they were not considered heroes back home. They were considered religious fanatics and potential troublemakers—with good reason. The governments of Egypt, Algeria, Libya, Syria, and Iraq had long been targeted by Islamic militants. They wanted to replace these governments with governments that follow and enforce strict Sharia law as they interpreted it.[7]

In June 1989 the African country of Sudan (see map on page 11) was taken over by a Muslim radical named Hasan al-Turabi. Sudan was considered a poor country with little appeal to visitors. But Turabi wanted to transform Sudan into a kind of Muslim paradise. So he invited all Muslims, regardless of their nationalities. Naturally, many *mujahideen* with no place else to go drifted to Sudan.[8]

Bin Laden returned to Saudi Arabia in November 1989. On one visit in 1990, the war hero was invited to make a speech at a Saudi mosque. He chose this moment to make his first known anti-American speech. He asked Arabs to cut off all ties with the U.S. people, even to refuse to buy U.S. products. "We have to make a stand against America because it helps Israel," he said.[9]

ANGERING THE KING

Two events in 1990 would soon turn bin Laden into an outcast in his own country. The first was peace in neighboring Yemen, the home of his father. The second was Iraq's brutal invasion of Kuwait, another neighbor, in August 1990.

The Yemenis were uniting after decades of civil war. But bin Laden disapproved of the new Republic of Yemen. Its government included people who sympathized with the Soviet Union. Bin Laden soon began financing an underground war against the new government. Yemeni agents left his house in Jeddah with suitcases full of cash. Bin Laden also traveled to Yemen and spoke at mosques. He criticized the new government and urged people to oppose it.[10]

However, the Saudi government favored the Yemeni peace. Saudi King Fahd told bin Laden to stay out of Yemen's business. But bin Laden refused. So the king, unaccustomed to being disobeyed, came down hard on bin Laden. He had the former hero called before the minister of the interior. Bin Laden was threatened with punishment and ordered to surrender his passport. That meant he could no longer travel outside Saudi Arabia.[11]

"We will fight him with faith."
—Osama bin Laden, talking about
Iraqi leader Saddam Hussein's
invasion of Kuwait, 1991

THE INVASION OF KUWAIT

This run-in with the royal family was minor compared to what happened over Kuwait. Bin Laden had long been a critic of Iraqi dictator Saddam

Hussein. He did not believe that Saddam was a real Muslim. Long before 1990, he warned people that Saddam had plans to invade Kuwait and Saudi Arabia. With those countries in his hands, Saddam would control most of the world's oil supply. But bin Laden's warnings only annoyed King Fahd further. At the time, the relationship between Saudi Arabia and Iraq was friendly. Saddam was hugely popular among Arabs.

All that changed on August 2, 1990, when Saddam's tanks rolled into defenseless Kuwait (see map on page 11). The Saudi government panicked. The Saudi army was well equipped. But the desert kingdom had a tiny population—smaller than that of New York City—and a tiny army to match. It could not hold back Saddam, who had the largest army in the Middle East.[12]

Only the U.S. Army could match Saddam's. But that posed a huge problem for King Fahd. The U.S. Army was made up of non-Muslims. Inviting these **infidels**—unbelievers—to the home of Mecca and Medina was seen as a deep insult to Islam by conservative Muslims. Bin Laden begged the king's intelligence chief not to invite the Americans. He told the official that he could raise a huge Muslim army to defend Saudi Arabia.

"There are no caves in Kuwait," the official told him. "What will you do when he [Saddam] lobs missiles at you with chemical and biological weapons?"

"We will fight him with faith," bin Laden responded.[13]

INFIDELS IN THE HOLY LAND

King Fahd ignored bin Laden's offer. Instead, he invited the Americans as well as soldiers from 33 other countries to defend Saudi Arabia. The Coalition, as this group of countries was called, prepared to drive Saddam out of Kuwait. In February and March 1991, Saddam's army

What is bin Laden like?

Many people have had contact with Osama bin Laden over the years. Most mention a few of the same things. He is over 1.8 meters (6 feet) tall and is very soft-spoken and quiet. Other than that, opinions differ. Abdel Bari Atwan, the editor of an Arab-language newspaper who interviewed bin Laden in the late 1990s, said:

> To be honest, the man is likable. He is really nice. You don't see him as somebody who will be the arch-terrorist, who will be the most dangerous man in the world. He doesn't strike you as charismatic. You are with somebody who you feel you knew for maybe ten or fifteen years, you don't feel a stranger when you meet him for the first time. . . . You feel he is shy. He doesn't look at you eye to eye. Usually when he talks to you he talks by looking down. His clothes are very, very humble, very simple.[14]

Peter Jouvenal, a CNN cameraman who filmed an interview in 1997, remembered:

> I just remember this rather limp sort of handshake. Not a proper handshake. I remember his hands were cold, like sort of shaking hands with a fish.[15]

Safiwullah, an Afghan man who was 15 years old when he lived next door to bin Laden in the late 1990s, remarked:

> It was very hard to see Osama; you couldn't see him. He came here in four-wheel drives with blacked-out windows. Arab guards patrolled around here at night. They didn't hire locals as guards or cooks. It was a secret place. They checked anybody coming by. Osama is a very nice guy. He's a great holy warrior. Why do they say he's a murderer and a bad guy? Osama is a hero.[16]

was sent reeling by the Coalition attack launched from Saudi Arabia. Saddam still held on to power, but he was never again a threat to nearby countries.

The Persian Gulf War, as the conflict was called, marked a turning point in bin Laden's relations with his native land. Bin Laden had generally been a patriotic Saudi. He refused to hear criticism of the royal family from other Muslim radicals. But now his opinion changed. He saw the Saudi government as no better than the governments of Egypt, Iraq, Syria, and other countries that did not follow Islam closely. He began secretly planning for the Saudi government's downfall. ❖

Headlines from 1992–1996

Here are some major news stories from the years of al Qaeda's first terrorist attacks.

Breakup of Yugoslavia Leads to Bosnian War

Like many former communist countries, Yugoslavia split apart when the former government fell in the early 1990s. In 1992 a complicated three-way war broke out among Serbs, Croats, and Muslims in the Bosnia region. All three ethnic groups had gotten along for decades. There had even been a lot of intermarriage. But people within each group inflamed old passions. All sides committed horrible murders, but the Serbs carried out the largest **massacres**.

Internet Usage Soars

The Internet is a global system of computer networks that exchange information. In the 1980s, it was still basically a tool of academics and military experts. In July 1992 Delphi became the first Internet service to offer services like e-mail to the public. Internet usage soared. The Internet quickly became a widespread tool for communication and research.

Rwanda Genocide Kills Thousands

For 100 days in 1994, the small African country of Rwanda became a killing field. Tensions between two groups, the Hutu and Tutsi, had always been strong. The Hutu-led government encouraged groups to begin attacking Tutsis. No Tutsi was safe. Between 500,000 and 1 million men, women, and children were killed.

Terrorist Attack Rocks Oklahoma City

On April 19, 1995, a truck bomb blew up a U.S. government office building in Oklahoma City, killing 168 and wounding 800. The three bombers were extremely conservative Americans who were angry with the U.S. government. At the time, this was the worst terrorist attack in the history of the United States, and it remains the worst terrorist attack carried out by U.S. citizens.

Israeli Prime Minister Yitzhak Rabin Assassinated

Hope for peace in the Middle East faded after an Israeli man shot and killed Israeli Prime Minister Yitzhak Rabin on November 4, 1995. The assassin opposed Rabin's efforts to make peace with the Palestinians (see page 23).

U.S. president Bill Clinton was among the hundreds of mourners attending the funeral of Yitzhak Rabin. The prime minister was shot as he left a peace rally, which had been attended by about 100,000 Israelis who supported his efforts to make peace with Palestinians. He was shot by 27-year-old Yigal Amir.

Al Qaeda Declares War

Osama bin Laden got his passport back from Saudi officials after important friends intervened on his behalf. He was then able to travel. He flew first to Pakistan and then, in 1992, to Sudan. He planned to start all over.[1]

Bin Laden's five years in Sudan were perhaps the most peaceful and happy of his life. He was a millionaire in one of the poorest countries on Earth. He brought with him bulldozers and earth-moving equipment. He announced plans to build a 300-kilometer (190-mile) road as a gift to the nation. Sudan's leaders welcomed him at the airport with flowers.[2]

At the time, bin Laden was virtually the only rich foreigner interested in investing in Sudan. The country was engaged in civil war. The Arab Muslim north was at war with the black, Christian south. Bin Laden bought a large three-story house for his huge family in the capital of Khartoum. About 1,000 al Qaeda members joined him there. But bin Laden seemed more interested in business ventures at first.[3]

BUILDING AND FARMING

Bin Laden began building—not just one road, but several. The government had little cash, so it paid him mostly in land. He became one of the country's largest landholders. He was also given a tannery for making fine leather goods. He owned several farms that produced everything from watermelons to chickens to sunflowers. He said that Sudan could feed the world if it were managed correctly.[4]

Bin Laden patterned himself after his father. He was a foreigner living in a poor country and becoming an important businessman. However, bin Laden's time in Sudan showed just how different he was from his father. Muhammad bin Laden rose from rags to riches by watching his businesses closely and making sure they turned a profit. Osama bin Laden let others run his businesses and told them that profit was not the most important thing. He lost a small fortune over time, as most of his ventures failed.[5]

Bin Laden also had some personal failures in Sudan. His insistence on a plain—even poor—lifestyle finally drove one wife and some of his children away. When bin Laden moved to Sudan, his wife Umm Ali asked for a divorce. She preferred the luxuries of Saudi Arabia. Bin Laden reluctantly granted it.

Two of bin Laden's oldest sons, Abdullah and Omar, also disliked living in poverty in Sudan. They had spent time with rich cousins in Saudi Arabia. Now teenagers, they missed having fast cars, televisions, and other modern conveniences. Both of them pushed to return to Saudi Arabia. Again, bin Laden grudgingly gave in, but he seldom mentioned those sons' names again.

LIFE IN SUDAN

Bin Laden lived a quiet life in Sudan. Each morning he walked to his local mosque to pray. A small crowd of admirers always followed him. He wore Sudanese dress, including a white turban and a white tunic called a *gallabea*. Sometimes he took his sons for picnics on the shores of the Nile River. Al Qaeda at this time became more of a farming business than a terrorist group. After prayers on Friday, al Qaeda members formed two soccer teams and played each other. Several times bin Laden told people that he was ready to quit al Qaeda and become a farmer.[6]

NEW ENEMIES

But bin Laden was not ready to give up on his *jihad*. His old enemy, the Soviet Union, collapsed in 1991. But he was still angered that U.S. troops remained on the Arabian peninsula, the holy "Land of the Two Mosques" (Mecca and Medina). During the Persian Gulf War, the United States promised that U.S. troops would leave Saudi Arabia right after the war. However, neither the U.S. nor the Saudi governments saw an urgent need to make them leave. So they stayed.

Bin Laden had long hated the United States. He hated its support for Israel and its support of non-Islamic leaders in Muslim countries. But more than anything, bin Laden and his followers hated "western culture," the lifestyle found in places like the United States, Europe, and Australia. The foundation of western culture is personal freedom— freedom to speak out, freedom to wear whatever one likes, and freedom to worship as one chooses. Americans and other westerners also take rapid technological change for granted. They adapt to new inventions like television and the Internet quickly.

"Music is the flute of the devil."
—Osama bin Laden

Most Muslims embrace these parts of western culture as well. In fact, tolerance and exploration have long been features of Islamic history. But Muslim radicals like bin Laden see this lifestyle as a huge threat to their beliefs. It requires tolerating people with different religions and different values. It means respecting the rights of religious minorities and giving greater freedom to women. It clashes head-on with their view of the world.[7]

Bin Laden's ideas were rigidly fixed, and this was obvious even in conservative Sudan. As a lifelong horse lover, he began attending horse races at Khartoum's racetrack. But life at the track was rowdy, with a lot of singing and dancing. Bin Laden first plugged his ears when songs played. Then he asked people to stop singing, a request they ignored. Finally, he stopped going to the races. "Music," he said, "is the flute of the devil."[8]

SPREADING TERROR

Bin Laden continued to welcome recruits to his terrorist training camps. The camps could be found in both Afghanistan and Sudan. Bin Laden welcomed all of those in Sudan with the same speech. He told them that the United States appeared to be very strong, but history showed that Americans always run from a real fight. He pointed out that the United States pulled out of Vietnam. He also talked about the 1983 bombing of a Marine barracks in Lebanon (see page 32).[9]

Al Qaeda launched some of its first small-scale attacks during these years. At the same time, bin Laden gave money to other radical Islamic groups that fought independently. Graduates from his terrorist camps were also able to attack targets independently. This way, attacks could be planned and carried out against al Qaeda's enemies without bin Laden's direct supervision. This was how bin Laden attempted to slowly turn al Qaeda into a global network of radical Muslim terrorism.

The following are some of the earliest acts of terrorism inspired by bin Laden and al Qaeda:

November 1991: An al Qaeda assassin attempted to stab to death the 77-year-old king of Afghanistan. The king barely survived the attack. The king had been living in exile in Italy. Al Qaeda disliked his moderate views. Bin Laden apparently feared that the king would return to Afghanistan and take over. This is considered al Qaeda's first terrorist attack.[10]

Early 1992: Bin Laden gave financial support to a radical Islamic group trying to overthrow the government of Algeria, in northwest Africa. With that aid, the group launched a bloody five-year civil war. The group often murdered whole villages full of innocent civilians in the middle of the night. After one massacre, the group's newspaper ran a headline that read: "Thank God! We have cut 200 throats today!" The government gradually stamped out the rebellion after about a decade of fighting. More than 100,000 people died.[11]

December 1992: U.S. President George H. W. Bush sent 28,000 U.S. troops to the African country of Somalia, in east Africa. Originally, they were there to feed starving Somalis. Later, the United States was drawn into fighting among rival **warlords**. Al Qaeda saw this as another attempt by the United States to take over a Muslim country. Bin Laden sent agents to inflame the Somalis to attack the Americans. But this proved to be unnecessary. Somalis attacked a group of U.S. soldiers, killing 19. These deaths made the mission unpopular, and the United States quickly withdrew its troops. This reinforced one of bin Laden's key beliefs about Americans—that they would run from a real fight.[12]

December 29, 1992: An al Qaeda bomb exploded at a hotel in Aden, Yemen. The bomb was aimed at U.S. soldiers who were visiting, but they had already left. Instead the bomb killed an Austrian tourist and a Yemeni hotel worker.[13]

February 26, 1993: The World Trade Center, located in the financial district of New York City, was bombed for the first time. Bin Laden bankrolled a blind Muslim holy man named Sheikh Omar Abdul

Rahman. Rahman, an Egyptian who lived in the United States, urged his followers to commit terrorist acts. One of them was Ramzi Yousef, a graduate of bin Laden's training camps. Yousef created a huge truck bomb and exploded it under the World Trade Center. If the bomb had been slightly larger, Yousef would have toppled one or maybe both towers. As it was, the explosion still managed to kill 6 and injure 1,042 people. Yousef was eventually caught and imprisoned. Rahman was later imprisoned for another, even larger plot to blow up New York City landmarks.[14]

Why attack the World Trade Center?

Skyscrapers are a U.S. invention, and tall skyscrapers like the World Trade Center towers have traditionally been a source of U.S. pride. In 1993 Muslim terrorists selected the World Trade Center as a target in part because it was so well known and visible. The World Trade Center was also a symbol of the United States' economic power. Many Wall Street financial firms were housed there. Destroying them was seen as a blow to the country's wealth and status as a world power.[15] Later, in 2001, bin Laden would target the World Trade Center for a more strategic reason. He believed that the United States' power was unstable. If Americans were hit in a few "weak spots"—places like the Capitol building (representing political power), the Pentagon (military power), and the World Trade Center (economic power)—its power would crumble forever. "If it is hit in one hundredth of those [weak] spots," he said, "God willing, it will stumble, wither away and relinquish world leadership."[16]

Late 1993: In late 1993 a Sudanese general sold bin Laden what was supposed to be enriched uranium—a key ingredient in making nuclear weapons. The reddish substance that he bought was actually red mercury, which looks a lot like enriched uranium. Bin Laden was scammed for $10,000. But he continued to look for ways to produce nuclear weapons. He also wanted to produce chemical gases and biological weapons that could sicken or kill large numbers of people.[17]

CUTTING TIES

By 1994 the Saudi government was angry at bin Laden. Complaints poured in from other Arab countries about him financing radical activities. The Saudis first offered bin Laden a bribe. They would pay him hundreds of millions of dollars to return home, renounce the *jihad*, and apologize to King Fahd for his disobedience. When that did not work, they sent bin Laden's mother, his uncle, and childhood friends to reason with him.

Finally, the Saudis threatened to strip him of both his fortune and his Saudi citizenship. Bin Laden would be cut off from his family and his homeland forever. But he still refused. "They think that a Muslim may bargain on his religion," he said. A Saudi official came to take away bin Laden's Saudi passport. He threw it at the man and declared, "Take it, if having it dictates anything on my behalf!"[18]

An assassination attempt

On February 4, 1994, bin Laden barely escaped an assassination attempt. The attempt was made by a Muslim who was even more radical than he was. He considered bin Laden to be a traitor to Islam. It is possible that some country—perhaps even Saudi Arabia—had organized the failed attack.[19]

Shortly after this, bin Laden's family issued a statement in the Saudi press expressing "regret, denunciation, and condemnation for all acts that Osama bin Laden may have committed." The Saudis and the Egyptians pressured Sudan to throw out their troublesome guest. The Sudanese resisted at first, but found themselves more and more isolated. By 1996 the Sudanese leader told bin Laden he either had to keep silent or leave.[20]

By this time, bin Laden was in desperate financial shape. His money from Saudi Arabia had been cut off. His business ventures in Sudan had almost all failed. The generous pay he had once given al Qaeda members was no longer possible. Bin Laden saw no other option. He had to leave Sudan. And the only country that would take him was Afghanistan, where he was still seen as a hero.[21]

A NEW HOME

Bin Laden arrived in Afghanistan in May 1996. He was broke. His family had disowned him. Many of his oldest friends and supporters had refused to follow him to Afghanistan. Bin Laden was also homesick. Despite his contempt for the Saudi government, he missed living in Saudi Arabia.

"The walls of oppression and humiliation cannot be demolished except in a rain of bullets. The freeman does not surrender leadership to infidels and sinners."
—Osama bin Laden, declaring war on the United States, 1996

At this moment, probably the lowest of his life, bin Laden decided to officially declare war on the United States. On August 23, 1996, he issued his declaration. It restated many of his old grievances, especially the presence of U.S. troops in Saudi Arabia. He said that Christians and Jews had spilled the blood of Muslims and must be stopped. "The walls of oppression and humiliation cannot be demolished except in a rain of bullets," he said. "The freeman does not surrender leadership to infidels and sinners."[22] Bin Laden's war had begun in earnest. ❖

At this anti-U.S. rally in the Pakistani city of Karachi, protestors declared their support for Osama bin Laden and the Taliban.

HEADLINES FROM 1997–2000

Here are some major news stories from the years leading up to the September 11, 2001 attack.

Asia Gripped by Financial Crisis

In 1997 Asia was gripped by fears of an economic meltdown that affected the whole region. The problems started when Thailand's previously strong economy showed signs of weakness. The crisis soon spread to the rest of Southeast Asia and Japan. The United States had to bail out several countries in order to keep the crisis from spreading worldwide.

Y2K Problem No Problem at All

For years experts warned that January 1, 2000, could be a day of disaster. Older computers were not set up to read dates that went past 1999. People feared that the change in calendar could cause many computers to simply stop working. This was called the Y2K problem. However, the bugs were sorted out long before New Year's Day in 2000. No significant problems were reported.

Human Genome Mapped

In June 2000 scientists announced that they had mapped the chemical instructions that make up human DNA. They also continued to work on the structure and function of the human body's 20,000 to 25,000 genes. With this information, scientists were able to create new tests and new drugs for previously untreatable diseases.

Bush Wins Close 2000 Presidential Election

In November 2000 Republican George W. Bush defeated Democrat Al Gore to become U.S. president, even though Gore won more popular votes. After a long recount, Bush won a slim majority in the Electoral College, which decides the outcome of the presidential race.

George W. Bush and his wife Laura wave to supporters. Bush's narrow win over Democratic candidate Al Gore came after a fierce contest. The Electoral College voted Bush into office, giving him 271 votes over Gore's 267. This marked the first time in more than a century that the Electoral College vote had gone against the popular vote in a U.S. presidential election.

Al Qaeda Strikes

*Osama bin Laden returned to Afghanistan at a lucky time for him. The country's grueling civil war was drawing to a close. A group of militant radicals, known as the **Taliban**, had recently taken control of most of the country. The Taliban won in part because it had financial support from both Pakistan and Saudi Arabia. Both countries wanted to impose their own strict version of Islam on other countries.*

The Taliban's leader was Mullah Mohammed Omar. He had lost an eye while fighting the Soviets. After the Soviets left, he became angry at the chaos that followed. He believed that the Prophet Mohammed spoke to him, telling him to bring peace to the country. Omar began recruiting students, or *taliban* in the local language, to become his fighters. In time, he declared himself "the ruler of all the Muslims."[1]

With foreign aid, the Taliban fulfilled Omar's dream of bringing peace. Afghans desperate to end the fighting accepted the Taliban's rule. But the price was high. The Taliban soon launched a religious reign of terror. Much of it was aimed at women. For instance, the Taliban banned women from any work or schooling outside the home. In Afghanistan, many women were the heads of families. The men had been killed in the fighting. Without work, these women and their families starved.

HARSH RULE

The Taliban also cracked down on anything fun or modern. The Taliban's forbidden list included kite flying, computers, VCRs, movies, television, chess, nail polish, firecrackers, and sewing catalogues. They also banned any book other than the Qu'ran. Men had to grow their beards long. Those who did not—or those who did not show up for prayers at the mosque—were arrested. Most of the animals at the zoo that had survived the war were slaughtered. They were seen as a distraction from Islam.[2]

At the time, Mullah Omar did not know bin Laden. The Taliban had not invited bin Laden and had no loyalty to him. Omar asked the Saudis what he should do with this famous guest. The Saudis told Omar to watch bin Laden and keep him from making public statements. Yet neither the Taliban nor the Saudis did anything, even after bin Laden's declaration of war against the United States.

Within the Taliban, some argued that bin Laden was too much trouble. They wanted to get rid of him. Others argued to let him stay. They assumed that he was still a rich man who could help rebuild the country.[3]

A SIMPLE LIFE

Despite people's impressions of his riches, bin Laden was actually quite poor at this point. His family and followers lived at a rundown farm in Afghanistan. It did not even have running water, let alone electricity or other modern conveniences. At one point, they had only bread and pomegranates to eat. To bin Laden, this was very appealing. "We want a simple life," he told Mullah Omar.[4] Bin Laden's three wives at the time lived in three separate houses within the family compound.[5] But diseases like hepatitis and malaria were rampant on the farm. "This place is worse than a tomb," one of his followers wrote home.[6]

TALKING TO THE PRESS

Despite warnings from the Taliban, bin Laden had no intention of remaining silent. In March 1997 he gave his first television interview. It aired on CNN on May 10. Peter Bergen was a CNN producer who put the interview together. "[Bin Laden] was extremely soft-spoken," he said. "If you didn't know what he was saying, you would have thought he was talking about the weather, but when you read the transcript of his remarks they were full of rage and fury against the United States."[7]

> ## "You'll see them and hear about them in the media, God willing."
> —Osama bin Laden, talking about his future plans, 1997

Among other things, bin Laden accused the U.S. government of being "unjust, criminal, and tyrannical [having oppressive power]." He also declared that members of the Saudi royal family were no longer Muslims. If that were true, other Muslims would be free to kill them without punishment from God. This was because, according to some radical Muslims like bin Laden, a Muslim can kill another Muslim if he or she turns away from Islam. When asked about his future plans, bin Laden said, "You'll see them and hear about them in the media, God willing."[8]

This interview was the first of several press conferences and interviews that bin Laden gave in the coming months. In all of them, he threatened the United States. But al Qaeda still had done little in the way of terrorist activity, so it was widely ignored.

AL-ZAWAHIRI RETURNS

Bin Laden was soon rejoined by his old ally, Ayman al-Zawahiri. The doctor had been a leader of a group called al-Jihad. It was focused on creating a Muslim theocracy in Egypt. But Egypt's government arrested most of his fighters and stopped the movement. Like bin Laden, Zawahiri blamed the United States for the problems of Muslims. He

Taliban fighters stand guard over men who are suspected of committing crimes. The men were accused of dressing up as Taliban fighters and trying to kidnap people for ransom money.

said Americans had waged a "war on God." He also said that "to kill the Americans and their allies—civilian and military—is an individual duty for every Muslim who can do it in any country in which it is possible to do it."[9]

THE EMBASSY BOMBINGS

On August 7, 1998, bin Laden finally backed up his words with actions. Al Qaeda launched its first true large-scale terrorist attacks. Suicide bombers placed trucks full of explosives near the U.S. embassies in the African countries of Kenya and Tanzania.[10]

The first truck bomb went off in Nairobi, Kenya's capital (see map on page 11). Many people standing near the windows were cut to pieces by flying glass.[11]

The bombing killed 213 people; 12 of them were Americans. More than 4,500 were injured, many by flying glass.[12]

Nine minutes later, a similar truck bomb went off near the U.S. embassy in Dar es Salaam, Tanzania's capital. But the truck was not able to get close to the target building. The suicide bombers' planned path was blocked by another truck. The mammoth explosion killed 11 and wounded 85. All of them were Africans.

THE U.S. RESPONSE

The attacks horrified most people, including most Muslims. Bin Laden quickly denied any involvement. But when one of the Nairobi bombers was interrogated by **Federal Bureau of Investigation (FBI)** agents, he quickly linked things back to bin Laden.

Ten days after the embassy bombings, the United States hit back. U.S. President Bill Clinton ordered long-range missile strikes to get back at bin Laden. But these strikes failed. Thirteen missiles were fired at a factory in Khartoum, Sudan, destroying it. The CIA had evidence that the factory was making chemical weapons for al Qaeda. However, it turned out that the plant actually made medicines. It had nothing to do with bin Laden.[13]

At the same time, U.S. ships fired 66 missiles at al Qaeda training camps in Afghanistan. The FBI and CIA had reason to believe that bin Laden and his Egyptian counselor Ayman al-Zawahiri would both be at a camp. Bin Laden almost was. A last-minute decision to go to Kabul, Afghanistan's capital, probably saved his life.[14]

The strikes destroyed the camps and killed a few men. But the camps were easily rebuilt. The failed U.S. attack turned bin Laden into a hero among many Muslims. "By the grace of God, I am alive!" he announced on the radio. Even kids in Kenya and Tanzania—the two countries that al Qaeda bombed—could be seen wearing Osama bin Laden T-shirts.[15]

> *"By the grace of God, I am alive!"*
> —Osama bin Laden, speaking after the
> United States launched an unsuccessful
> missile attack to kill him, 1998

SWEARING ALLEGIANCE

At this point, Saudi Arabia and Pakistan demanded that bin Laden be handed over to them by the Taliban (see pages 66–67). At first, Mullah Omar was inclined to agree. But he had a problem. Handing over such a famous guest would make him look weak. Bin Laden chose this time to take advantage of the Afghan warlord's ego. Bin Laden swore *bayat* to Mullah Omar. *Bayat* is a religiously binding oath of allegiance. After this, Mullah Omar became bin Laden's most loyal supporter.[16]

A FOILED PLOT

The year 1999 was an anxious one for U.S. officials. Many people were excited about the year 2000. It would mark the start of a new millennium—a 1,000-year period. New Year's Day was expected to be especially festive. Officials worried that terrorists would use those festivities to launch a high-profile attack.

On December 14, 1999, a border guard at Port Angeles, Washington, stopped a suspicious-looking man. The man, an Algerian named Ahmed Ressam, seemed extremely nervous. A quick check of his trunk revealed it was full of explosive chemicals and timers—materials used to make bombs. Ressam's target had been Los Angeles International Airport. He was not working under orders from bin Laden. But he had been through bin Laden's training camps and used this training to form his own terrorist group. (He planned to give bin Laden credit for the bombing, if he wanted it.) One alert border guard may have saved hundreds, perhaps thousands, of lives.[17]

THE USS *COLE* BOMBING

In January 2000 al Qaeda planned to blow up a U.S. warship as it refueled in Aden, Yemen's capital (see map on page 11). But the bomb-maker overloaded the small fiberglass boat with explosives, and the boat sank.[18]

Al Qaeda retrieved the boat and prepared it for another mission. On October 7, 2000, two al Qaeda suicide bombers piloted their bomb-laden boat beside the USS *Cole*, again in Aden. The bomb ripped a giant hole in the ship's side, almost causing it to sink. The blast killed 17 U.S. sailors and wounded 39 others.[19]

The bomb used to attack the USS Cole *consisted of an estimated 272 kilograms (600 pounds) of high explosives, and punched a 12-meter (39-foot) hole in the side of the ship. Many terrorism experts agreed that this attack represented a significant technical advance from other terrorist attacks, such as the U.S. embassy bombings in Africa (see page 69) two years earlier.*

Severely damaging a U.S. warship seemed heroic to many Muslims. More men than ever flocked to bin Laden's training camps. More importantly, money poured in from individuals in oil-rich states like Qatar and Bahrain. Al Qaeda had a huge supply of money once again. Some of it would be used to bankroll bin Laden's most ambitious scheme yet. He was finally going to attack the United States itself.[20] ❖

Bin Laden the poet

Bin Laden likes to read, memorize, and write poetry. In fact, some of the video messages that he releases from time to time feature him reciting his own poetry. He read this poem before about 500 people at the wedding of his 17-year-old son Muhammad in early 2001. It praises the attack on the USS *Cole*:

> A destroyer: even the brave fear its might.
> It inspires horror in the harbor and in the open sea
> She sails into the waves
> Flanked by arrogance, haughtiness, and false power.
> To her doom she moves slowly
> A dinghy [small boat] awaits her, riding the waves.

Princeton professor Bernard Haykel says bin Laden's use of poetic language helps explain his ongoing popularity in the Arabic-speaking world. Arab culture puts a high value on poetic language. Speaking in this way allows bin Laden to make himself look like Arab heroes of the past.[21]

HEADLINES FROM 2001

Here are some major news stories from the days before the September 11 terrorist attacks.

News of U.S. Shark Attacks Overblown, Critics Say

A series of stories about shark attacks frightened many Americans off the beaches in the summer of 2001. In early September a 10-year-old boy was attacked and killed off a beach in Virginia, while a 23-year-old woman was killed off a North Carolina beach. Even so, ocean scientists said that shark activity was no higher than normal. Instead, they said, the news media blew the problem out of proportion.

Most Nations Condemn Election in Belarus

Most countries condemned the September 9, 2001, reelection of President Aleksandr Lukashenko as leader of Belarus, a country in eastern Europe. Western human rights groups said that Lukashenko rigged the election. He kept opposition voters from registering their votes, and he forced the news media to write negative stories about his opponents. Russia, which was friendly with Belarus, was one of the few countries to support the election results.

Violence Spreads in Middle East, Despite Plans for Talks

On September 10, 2001, Israeli and Palestinian leaders made plans to sit down and talk about peace. But the undeclared war between them continued (see page 23). Palestinian snipers killed two Israeli soldiers. Meanwhile, Israeli tanks shelled Palestinian positions. The shelling killed a Palestinian policeman and wounded four others.

Suicide Bomber Kills Two Police Officers in Turkey

Police believed that a communist group set off a suicide bomb in a busy market in Istanbul, Turkey's largest city, on September 10, 2001. The bomber, who may have been a woman, killed two Turkish police officers and wounded twenty others. The bombing was probably to protest conditions in Turkish prisons. Many Turkish communists were arrested.

Biden Attacks Bush's Missile Shield Idea

Democratic U.S. Senator Joe Biden criticized Republican President George W. Bush for his push to build a missile shield (a network of radar, missiles and satellites designed to detect and destroy nuclear missiles). Bush said that such a shield would protect the United States against nuclear missile attack. The president made it one of his top priorities. On September 10, 2001, Biden pointed out that U.S. military leaders believed that such a missile attack is much less likely than "a region conflict, a major [ground] war, terrorist attacks at home or abroad or any number of other real issues."

September 11

The first stage of bin Laden's September 11, 2001, attacks actually took place on September 9. And it did not happen in the United States. It took place in Afghanistan. Bin Laden did a favor for his friend and patron Mullah Omar. He had someone killed. Ahmad Shah Massoud was the leader of the Northern Alliance, a coalition of Afghan warlords who opposed the Taliban. Massoud was a clever military leader and the biggest threat to the Taliban's rule. Like bin Laden, Massoud did interviews with the press. On September 9, two of bin Laden's suicide bombers got close to the well-protected Massoud by posing as reporters. A bomb hidden in their camera killed the Northern Alliance leader.

Bin Laden had removed the Taliban's last obstacle to controlling Afghanistan. But he had also done himself some good. Massoud would have been a valuable ally to the United States after the September 11 bombings. That is because bin Laden's main goal was not just to blow up U.S. buildings or ships.

Osama bin Laden thought that the attack on the embassies and the USS *Cole* would trigger a U.S. invasion of Afghanistan. In November 2000 he explained his strategy to a reporter. Bin Laden said, "We did the [USS] *Cole* attack and we wanted the United States to react. And if they reacted,

This security film still shows one of the 9-11 hijackers (the man in the blue shirt) walk right through the screening checkpoint.

The suicide bombers

The men who carried out the September 11 attacks came from a variety of backgrounds. Fourteen of the nineteen were from Saudi Arabia. Two were from United Arab Emirates. One was from Lebanon. And another was from Egypt. (See map on page 11.) Several, like Mohammed Atta, had earned college degrees or taken some classes. Many had lived in either the United States or Europe and seemed to blend in well.[1]

The nineteen suicide bombers were split into four teams.[2] The plan was simple. Each man carried either a small knife or a box cutter. Some of them also carried mace or pepper spray. At the time, airport security was so lax that it was easy to get these items on board. The men used their weapons to overpower the flight crew. Four of the men had spent several months in flight school in the United States (paid for by bin Laden). They acted as the pilots and flew the planes into their targets.[3]

All of the September 11 bombers believed that their acts would lead them immediately to paradise. The instructions given to the hijack teams reminded them to not be afraid: "[Your death] will begin a happy and contented life and immortal blessings with the prophets, the true ones, and the righteous martyrs."[4]

they are going to invade Afghanistan, and that's what we want. We want them to come to our country. . . . And then we will start holy war against the Americans, exactly like the Soviets."[5] Bin Laden believed that a bloody holy war in Afghanistan would help destroy the United States.

Instead, the United States responded by catching and punishing the men who had committed the crimes. On May 29, 2001, a New York jury voted to convict four men of helping with the embassy bombings. The FBI was conducting a similar investigation to find the surviving plotters in the USS *Cole* bombing.[6] So bin Laden pinned his hopes on another, more ambitious operation.

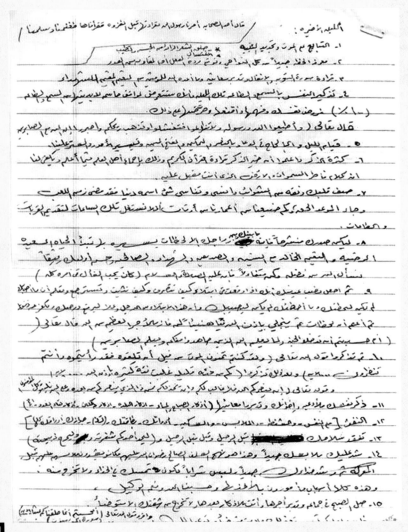

This is one of several letters, handwritten in Arabic, containing instructions to the 9/11 hijackers as well as Islamic prayers. Among other things, the letter tells the hijackers to be sure that they know the plan, and also contains a pledge of allegiance to death. This letter provided the first public evidence the U.S. released linking 3 of the 19 suspected hijackers.

The people tracking bin Laden

The United States was slow to respond to the threat posed by Osama bin Laden. Part of the problem was the usual secretiveness of Muslim terrorists. But language also played a role. The FBI and CIA had few reliable Arabic translators. Americans were largely unaware of what this Arabic-speaking terrorist was saying.

The FBI and CIA knew that foreign terrorists might attack Americans overseas. But few experts foresaw a serious attack on U.S. soil. In 1996 the CIA finally set up Alec Station. This was a bureau designed specifically to track bin Laden and al Qaeda. The FBI and CIA agents who studied bin Laden took him very seriously. But they still had trouble convincing their superiors of the danger he posed.

There was another problem: The two agencies did not get along well. The FBI's job was to bring criminals to justice in the United States. The CIA's job was to gather intelligence overseas. Agents carrying out those different jobs clashed frequently. Likewise, they did not get along well with the National Security Agency (NSA), which monitors international communications.

Agents on all sides concealed information from one another. The CIA was especially bad about passing on vital intelligence. Had these agencies cooperated more, bin Laden would probably never have pulled off the attack on September 11.[7]

THE PLAN

In 1996, a follower named Khalid Sheikh Mohammed had come to bin Laden with a plan to hijack 10 airplanes and crash them into buildings all over the world. Bin Laden gave Mohammed the go-ahead for a similar plan in the spring of 1999, making him the attack's chief planner.[8] Bin Laden personally handled two important details about September 11. He helped choose the buildings to be targeted. He also chose the man who would become the lead hijacker, Muhammad Atta. Otherwise he left other planning matters to Mohammed and Atta.[9]

MOUNTING THREATS

In the United States, **counterterrorism** officials could feel that something big was brewing. Among other things, the FBI had gotten reports that al Qaeda was planning a "Hiroshima" in the United States. Hiroshima was the first city to be destroyed by an atomic bomb. The bomb was dropped by the United States during World War II.

Agents at different agencies had tips that al Qaeda was up to something. There were warnings from Egypt and Afghanistan. One tip even alerted the FBI that airplanes might be used as flying bombs. An agent tried to sound the alarm about this. But between January and September 2001, the FBI alone received more than 1,000 threats. There were not enough agents to investigate them all.[10]

Richard Clarke was the head of counterterrorism for the National Security Council. On July 5, 2001, Clarke assembled the heads of several important departments. They included the Coast Guard, the Secret Service, and the Federal Aviation Administration. "Something really spectacular is going to happen here, and it's going to happen soon," he said.[11]

NOT A PRIORITY

The previous January, the United States had elected a new president— George W. Bush. Clarke tried to warn Bush about the threat that al Qaeda posed to the United States. But neither Bush nor his top advisors seemed interested. They were far more concerned about fighting illegal drugs and building a missile-defense system. Bush even downgraded Clarke's position—a sign that counterterrorism was not a priority.[12]

Later investigations would show that the hijackers left plenty of clues. But the lack of cooperation among U.S. intelligence agencies kept them from putting the pieces of the puzzle together. The lack of interest from top-level officials kept the agencies from working together.[13]

FLIGHT	PASSENGERS AND CREW	BOUND FOR	HIJACKER TARGET
American Airlines Flight 11	92	Los Angeles	World Trade Center north tower
United Flight 175	65	Los Angeles	World Trade Center south tower
American Airlines Flight 77	64	Los Angeles	Pentagon
United Flight 93	45	San Francisco	Probably the U.S. Capitol building, but the plane crashed in Shanksville, Pennsylvania

OUT OF A CLEAR BLUE SKY

September 11 turned out to be a glorious fall morning in New York City and Washington, D.C. The air was cool but comfortable. The sky was a deep, clear color of blue. It was perfect flying weather.

On four planes headed cross-country from the East Coast, 19 hijackers went into action. Using low-tech weapons such as box cutters, they took control of the planes. They planned to use them as "missiles" to destroy well-known buildings in New York and Washington, D.C.

American Airlines Flight 11 became the first plane to make impact. It crashed into the north tower of the World Trade Center at 8:47 a.m. Relatively few people witnessed the first collision. But dozens of television cameras were focused on the World Trade Center when the second plane, United Flight 175, hit the south tower at 9:02.[14]

WHAT HAPPENED NEXT

For the next hour and a half, bin Laden's attack against the United States horrified television viewers around the world.

- At 9:41 a.m., American Airlines Flight 77 crashed into the Pentagon, in Washington, D.C. The explosion from the fuel-laden plane tore a massive hole into the U.S. military headquarters. It killed 125 people.

- At 9:50, high temperatures created by the burning jet fuel caused the World Trade Center's south tower to abruptly collapse. Hundreds of police, firefighters, and civilians were still in the building.

- At 10:00, United Airlines Flight 93 crashed in a field outside Shanksville, Pennsylvania. By using cell phones and talking to people on the ground, the passengers had found out that their plane was to be used as a flying bomb. They rushed the hijackers to stop them, which apparently caused the crash. This plane was supposed to crash into the U.S. Capitol building or the White House in Washington, D.C.

- At 10:28 the north tower of the World Trade Center collapsed like the south tower did, leaving only a giant column of smoke and dust.[15]

A SHOCKING DAY

In both New York City and Washington, D.C., people walked around stunned the rest of the day. Nothing was as it should have been. Theaters and restaurants shut down. Subways and buses did not run. That forced huge crowds of people into the streets. Most commercial air traffic would be grounded for the next two days.[16] But every so often a military jet fighter screamed across the sky. Crowds of people ducked at the sound. They thought another attack was coming.[17]

Most Americans asked the same questions. How did a bunch of men with knives and box cutters do this? How are we going to fight back? ❖

Who died on September 11?

The September 11 attack on the United States killed 2,973 people.[18] Most of the victims were Americans. They came from a broad geographic area, spanning at least 25 states.

But Americans did not suffer alone. Forty other countries were represented among the dead. They included 67 Britons, 23 Japanese, 17 Colombians, and 16 Jamaicans. There were also people from countries as far flung as Mexico (15), Australia (4), Israel (2), China (2), Ireland (1), Nigeria (1), and Indonesia (1).[19]

Most of the victims were in their mid- to late thirties. Men outnumbered women by about three to one.[20] After September 11, 17 women gave birth to children who lost their fathers in the attacks. The attacks turned 1,300 children into orphans. People who are exposed to violent events often suffer from post-traumatic stress disorder. It can cause many symptoms, including lack of sleep, flashbacks, emotional numbness, and even violence.[21] More than 400,000 New Yorkers were estimated to have the disorder after September 11, including 10,000 schoolchildren.[22]

HEADLINES FROM 2002–PRESENT

Here are some major news stories from the years bin Laden has been on the run.

The U.S. Invades Iraq

President George W. Bush directed U.S. troops to invade Iraq on March 20, 2003. U.S. leaders were convinced that Iraqi leader Saddam Hussein possessed weapons of mass destruction. They feared that those weapons would be given to terrorists. British Prime Minister Tony Blair supported the invasion. However, other traditional allies, such as France and Germany, did not.

March 11, 2004: Terrorists Bomb Madrid Trains, 191 killed, 1,841 wounded

Asian Tsunami Kills More Than 225,000

On December 26, 2004, an earthquake shook an area under the Indian Ocean near Indonesia. The earthquake triggered a giant tsunami—a massive wave. This swamped coastlines from Africa to Indonesia. The wave broke suddenly and killed more than 225,000 people. It was one of the deadliest natural disasters in recorded history.

A hard-hit area of Indonesia, in the aftermath of the 2004 tsunami. Indonesia was the hardest hit country, with an estimated 387,000 people left homeless, and more than 100,000 Indonesians killed.

Terrorist Bombers Attack London Underground

On the morning of July 7, 2005, London was celebrating its newly announced win over Paris for the right to host the 2012 Olympics. Then, as the morning rush period was ending, three bombs exploded on separate underground commuter trains. The bombs were detonated by suicide bombers, and came almost at the exact same moment. About an hour later, a fourth suicide bomber blew up a double decker bus. Fifty-two people were killed during these attacks, and more than 770 were injured.

The British Police conduct a forensic investigation of the bus explosion.

Catching bin Laden

Overnight, Osama bin Laden became the world's most wanted man. Everyone knew where to find him—in Afghanistan. But Mullah Omar would not hand him over. "I will not hand over a Muslim to an infidel," he declared.[1] President George W. Bush made it clear that Afghanistan risked invasion. "We will make no distinction between the terrorists who committed these acts and those who harbor them [give them a place to stay]," he said in a televised address.[2]

DISAPPOINTED

On October 7, 2001, the United States attacked Afghanistan. But the great battle bin Laden imagined against the Americans did not come about. The Americans sent bombers and a few hundred ground fighters. The Americans also re-armed and financed the Northern Alliance, a coalition of Afghan warlords who opposed the Taliban. The Alliance's 20,000 soldiers did most of the ground fighting.

Instead of waging holy war against infidel Americans, al Qaeda and Taliban fighters were up against fellow Muslims. This was a bitter disappointment. Meanwhile, bombs rained from U.S. warplanes. The holy warriors had no way to fight back against them.[3]

Controversial tactics

Following the September 11 attacks, President Bush launched a "War on Terror." This was a campaign to capture or kill al Qaeda members and anyone else who planned to use terrorism against the United States.

One of the most controversial tools in the War on Terror was the use of torture. Torture is inflicting physical or mental pain on someone, usually to get information. Torture is forbidden under U.S. and international law. Nevertheless, President Bush ordered U.S. military and intelligence agencies to use harsh methods of interrogation (methods that were widely considered to be torture), on al Qaeda suspects who were captured. The FBI refused to use torture. However, the CIA and military did use it.

Another controversial aspect of the War on Terror was the detention of prisoners at a U.S. military base at Guantánamo Bay, in Cuba. The U.S. Constitution calls for suspected criminals to get a speedy trial. By using the prison on foreign soil, U.S. officials argued that the al Qaeda suspects could be held indefinitely without ever going to trial. Other U.S. officials said that this—like torture—was a violation of U.S. law. The prison at Guantánamo Bay became a huge public relations problem for the U.S. government. As it became increasingly clear that many of the people being held at the prison had very little evidence against them, international and public pressure to close the prison became very strong.

U.S. policy toward al Qaeda suspects changed sharply once Bush left office in 2009. Bush's successor, Barack Obama, quickly ordered that the controversial interrogation methods allowed under Bush no longer be used, and made plans to close the prison at Guantánamo Bay.[4]

Bin Laden still hoped to spark a Muslim uprising against the Americans. He released a videotape that said "every Muslim should rush to defend his religion."[5] But Muslims ignored this call.

TORA BORA

Bin Laden decided to make a stand in the mountains of Tora Bora, in eastern Afghanistan. These were the mountains in which he had once fought against the Soviets.

The Americans pounded bin Laden's caves and trenches with bombs. The CIA had hired some Afghan warlords to lead the final attack to capture bin Laden at Tora Bora. But that proved to be a mistake. Some of the warlords were friendly to al Qaeda. In early December 2001, they let bin Laden, Zawahiri, and Mullah Omar escape over the border to Pakistan. There have been no reliable sightings of bin Laden since. The U.S. lost its best chance to kill or capture Osama bin Laden.[6]

SEARCHING FOR BIN LADEN

Since 2001 reporters have guessed several times that bin Laden is either dead or very ill. This is based on rumors that he suffers from a kidney disease. However, the rumors appear to be untrue. People who have known him say they never heard of any kidney illness. Bin Laden does have low blood pressure. He also suffered a foot wound while fighting against the Soviets and a severe shoulder wound in the battle at Tora Bora. And bin Laden's age is catching up with him. There are more gray hairs in his beard and hair. However, there is no reason to believe that bin Laden will soon die of natural causes.[7]

Bin Laden has released a series of videotapes and audiotapes to the Arabic press that prove he is not dead or seriously ill. So has his second in command, Zawahiri. These videos almost always contain the same elements. Bin Laden routinely criticizes the United States and Israel. He calls upon Muslims to rise up against those two countries.[8]

Bin Laden recorded this video from the caves of Afghanistan, while the Taliban was still in power. In the video he praised the September 11 attacks and defied the U.S. threats to attack the Taliban government. The U.S. overthrew the Taliban days later.

So where is bin Laden? The best guess is that he is hiding in western Pakistan. That region, often referred to as the tribal areas, is right on the border with Afghanistan (see map on page 11). The Pakistani government has little control there. Instead it is ruled by local warlords who have great sympathy for bin Laden's hatred of the United States and his brand of radical Islam.

However, nobody really knows where bin Laden is hiding. Many have guessed that he is living in caves, getting by on bread and water. However, his many videos paint another picture. They show that bin Laden is well fed and wearing clean clothes. He frequently refers to recent news events around the world. That shows that he has access to television stations like CNN, BBC, and Al-Jazeera.[9]

A HIGH PRICE

Bin Laden paid dearly for the September 11 attacks. He was driven from Afghanistan, the best base that al Qaeda ever had. In the fighting that followed, al Qaeda lost most of its fighters. The organization was virtually destroyed. Its camps were closed.

Before September 11, al Qaeda was funded in part by Islamic groups posing as charities. These charities worked in many different countries. Outrage over the attacks allowed the United States to demand that the charities be shut down. Most of them were. This cut off most funding for al Qaeda.

Also, the militant Taliban reign was replaced by a more moderate, democratically elected government. Though they were driven out of the government, the Taliban continue to wage a vicious fight against the U.S. and its allies in Afghanistan.

However, bin Laden can also claim some partial victories. One of his biggest demands was the removal of U.S. troops from "the land of the Two Mosques," the Arabian peninsula. In 2003 the United States quietly pulled virtually all its troops out of Saudi Arabia. However, it still has bases in other countries on the peninsula—Kuwait, Qatar, and Bahrain (see map on page 11).[10]

Muslim terrorists still look to bin Laden and Zawahiri for guidance. In 2002 bin Laden issued a tape calling for renewed attacks on the West. That October a disco in Bali, Indonesia, was bombed. The bomb killed 202 people, most of them Australian tourists. In September 2003, Zawahiri condemned Pakistani leader Pervez Musharraf for attacking al Qaeda. Three months later, Musharraf narrowly escaped two assassination attempts.[11]

GROWING INFLUENCE

Bin Laden's influence has also grown in Iraq. The United States invaded Iraq in 2003 as part of President Bush's War on Terror. Bush was concerned that Iraq had weapons of mass destruction, and that they might wind up in the hands of al Qaeda. As it turned out, Iraq had no weapons of mass destruction.

Saddam Hussein was removed from power and executed. But the presence of Americans in Iraq caused a new terrorist movement to gain steam. Many of those terrorists have pledged their support to bin Laden and al Qaeda. Rising U.S. troop levels have stopped many of the terrorist attacks in Iraq. But the war there has given valuable training to a new generation of Muslim terrorists.[12]

The war in Iraq also drained badly needed troops and funding from the war in Afghanistan. As a result, the Taliban has grown strong again. The feeble Afghan government has not been able to cope. Suicide bombers have become a common occurrence in the capital city of Kabul.[13] The U.S.-led Coalition forces are not planning to leave Afghanistan soon. But the occupation there has not ended the threat posed by the Taliban and al Qaeda.

POPULAR VS. UNPOPULAR

In the Muslim world, opinions about bin Laden are complicated. Most Muslims were horrified by the death and destruction of September 11. They spoke out forcefully against it. People have pointed out accurately that the Qu'ran forbids the killing of innocent people for any reason.

Many Muslims simply deny that any Arabs—including Osama bin Laden—were behind September 11 at all. This feeling is especially strong in the Middle East. In 2006 the Pew Global Attitudes Project asked Muslims in Europe, as well as those in Muslim countries, "Did Arabs carry out the 9/11 attacks?" A majority replied "no."[14]

However, any lingering doubts about bin Laden's guilt ended in October 2004. That is when he released a videotape in which he admitted for the first time that he organized the September 11 attacks.[15] This videotape joined a mountain of other evidence that already tied bin Laden directly to September 11.[16]

Bin Laden's popularity among Muslims swings wildly from country to country. According to a 2006 poll, Muslims in European countries like the United Kingdom and Spain gave him almost no support. But in Nigeria, which is in Africa, about 61 percent of the Muslims backed him. He also has strong support in countries like Pakistan and Indonesia. Why? He is probably supported because he has stood up to the powerful United States and other western countries.[17] Even so, bin Laden's popularity has dropped sharply among Muslims in the years since September 11.[18]

"The battle is between us and the enemies of Islam, and it will go on until the [final] Hour."
—Osama bin Laden, talking about his war against the United States and other western countries

---

NO EASY ENDING

Peter Bergen is a journalist who has covered bin Laden since the 1990s. He believes the struggle against bin Laden is likely to last many years. He says, "We have barely begun the war with al Qaeda and its affiliated groups because many thousands of underemployed, disaffected men in the Muslim world will continue to embrace bin Laden's doctrine [teachings] of violent anti-Westernism."[19]

But bin Laden and al Qaeda have a serious problem. Many Muslims share their anger at the United States. Yet they do not like what al Qaeda ultimately stands for—making all Muslim countries enforce extremist Muslim law as they interpret it. This does not appeal to most Muslims. They want more freedom, not less.[20]

Still, bin Laden will keep on fighting. And he has made two things clear. First, he will not be captured. "I swear not to die but [as] a free man," he has said.[21] Second, bin Laden has shown that there will be no peace until he gets his way. "The battle is between us and the enemies of Islam," he has said, "and it will go on until the [final] Hour."[22] ❖

STOP PRESS... STOP PRESS... STOP PRESS... STO

Los Angeles Times

MONDAY, MAY 2, 2011

75¢ DESIGNATED AREAS HIGHER 58 PAGES © 2011 EST

U.S. KILLS BIN LADEN

leader dies in a firefight near Pakista...
...has been done,' Obama say...

BOB DROGIN,
KEN DILANIAN
AND DAVID CLOUD
REPORTING FROM

As this book was about to be printed, bin Laden met his own final hour. On May 1, 2011, U.S. forces entered a house in Abbottabad, Pakistan, and shot dead the al Qaeda leader. President Barack Obama revealed bin Laden had been swiftly buried at sea. Details of the attack are still uncertain, as are the consequences of this military action. Many fear the violence will continue.

TOP PRESS... STOP PRESS... STOP PRESS... STO

Timeline

1957   Osama bin Laden is born in Riyadh, Saudi Arabia.

1963   U.S. President John F. Kennedy is assassinated.

1966   Muslim radical writer Sayyid Qutb is executed by Egypt, but his teachings spread widely after his death.

Chinese ruler Mao Zedong launches the Cultural Revolution.

1967   Arab nations and Israel fight the Six-Day War. Israel makes large territorial gains, including the city of Jerusalem. This is a huge blow to Arab pride.

Bin Laden's father Muhammad bin Laden dies in a plane crash.

1968   Bin Laden attends Al Thagr High School in Jeddah. Soon takes interest in Muslim Brotherhood and radical Islam.

1974   Bin Laden marries his first wife.

1979   Shah of Iran is overthrown. He is replaced by radical Muslim rulers.

Camp David peace talks bring peace between Israel and Egypt. This peace angers Muslim extremists.

Deposed Pakistani Prime Minister Zulfikar Ali Bhutto is executed after a coup by military dictatorship that strictly follows Muslim laws.

Radical Muslim students take over the U.S. embassy in Tehran, Iran, and hold hostages for 444 days with the government's approval.

A group of about 500 radical Muslims takes over Mecca's Grand Mosque, the holiest site in Islam. The fighting lasts for two weeks and kills at least 200 people.

Soviet invasion of Afghanistan

1980   Bin Laden makes his first trip to Pakistan in effort to help Afghan refugees and *mujahideen*.

Ronald Reagan elected U.S. president.

1983   A suicide bomber drives a truck full of explosives into a Marine base in Lebanon. The explosion kills 241 and prompts the United States to pull its troops out of Lebanon.

1984   Bin Laden makes his first trip inside Afghanistan to witness fighting.

1985   Mikhail Gorbachev becomes Soviet leader. He pursues more moderate policies that boost freedom of expression and economic freedom within the communist system.

1986   Bin Laden creates a military base at Jaji in Afghanistan.

1987   Battle of Jaji gives bin Laden a reputation as a fighter.

1988   Bin Laden founds al Qaeda.

1989	The Soviet Union pulls its troops out of Afghanistan. Afghanistan quickly lapses into civil war. Bin Laden returns to Saudi Arabia.
1990	Bin Laden makes his first anti-American speech.
	IRAQ INVADES KUWAIT. THIS PROMPTS SAUDI ARABIA TO INVITE U.S. AND OTHER NON-MUSLIM TROOPS ON SAUDI SOIL FOR PROTECTION.
1991	THE U.S.-LED COALITION FORCES DRIVE IRAQI ARMIES OUT OF KUWAIT. U.S. TROOPS REMAIN STATIONED IN SAUDI ARABIA TO PROTECT THE KINGDOM AGAINST ANY FUTURE ATTACKS.
1992	Bin Laden moves to Sudan. He begins backing radical Muslim terrorist activities throughout the Middle East.
1994	Bin Laden's family in Saudi Arabia disowns him because of his backing of terrorist activities. However, many suspect that family members still help him financially.
1995	A JEWISH EXTREMIST KILLS ISRAELI PRIME MINISTER YITZHAK RABIN. THE ASSASSIN OPPOSED RABIN'S EFFORTS TO MAKE PEACE WITH PALESTINIANS.
1996	Bin Laden is pressured to leave Sudan. He finally goes back to Afghanistan. Bin Laden declares war on the United States.
	Bin Laden hears a plan that eventually leads to the September 11 attack.
1997	Bin Laden makes his first televised interview on CNN. This begins a series of televised interviews in which Bin Laden makes threats against the United States and western countries.
1998	AL QAEDA OPERATIVES BOMB U.S. EMBASSIES IN KENYA AND TANZANIA. THE ATTACKS KILL 298.
	THE U.S. ARRESTS EGYPTIAN-AMERICAN ALI MOHAMED FOR BEING A SPY. MOHAMED SERVED IN THE U.S. ARMY AND PROVIDED AL QAEDA WITH MILITARY TRAINING AND U.S. MANUALS ON BOMB MAKING AND OTHER TERRORIST ACTIVITIES.
2000	AL QAEDA OPERATIVES BOMB THE USS *COLE* IN YEMEN, KILLING 17.
2001	ON SEPTEMBER 11, THREE U.S. AIRPLANES ARE HIJACKED AND FLOWN INTO THE WORLD TRADE CENTER IN NEW YORK AND THE PENTAGON IN WASHINGTON. A FOURTH HIJACKED PLANE CRASHES IN PENNSYLVANIA, APPARENTLY ON ITS WAY TO THE U.S. CAPITOL.
	U.S invades Afghanistan in response. Bin Laden escapes capture during the Battle of Tora Bora.
2004	Bin Laden takes responsibility for the September 11 attack in a video taped message. It is one of many video taped messages that bin Laden has released since the September 11 attacks.
2009	Bin Laden believed to be hiding in mountainous area of western Pakistan, but whereabouts are unknown.
2011	Osama bin Laden found and killed by U.S. forces in Abbottabad, Pakistan.

Glossary

Arab member of a group of people originally from the Arabian peninsula and neighboring areas. Arabs now live in most of the Middle East and North Africa.

Central Intelligence Agency (CIA) the United States' top overseas spy agency

civil war war between two organized groups for control of the same country or region, or to change a government policy

cleric official in a religion, such as a priest, minister, rabbi, or imam

coalition group in which different groups of people unite to work toward the same goal

Cold War mostly nonviolent—or "cold"—war that pitted the United States and its allies against the Soviet Union and its allies. It lasted from 1946 to 1991.

communist person or government that believes the government should own all property. In practice, this belief often leads to great limits on personal freedom.

counterterrorism political and military activities designed to prevent terrorism

devout totally committed to a cause or belief

dictatorship country ruled by a dictator, or absolute ruler

embassy official residence of an ambassador from a foreign country. It usually includes the ambassador's staff and offers services to people visiting from the ambassador's country, and issues visas to people who want to visit the ambassador's country.

fanatical single-minded focus on a goal or purpose

fatwa Islamic religious opinion or order, usually issued by a cleric or other religious scholar

Federal Bureau of Investigation (FBI) the United States' top crime-fighting agency at home. Part of its job is to track foreign spies and terrorists within the United States.

infidel term used by very religious people to describe those who do not believe in a particular religion

Islam religion focused on the worship of God, as revealed by the Prophet Muhammad in the 600s CE. Its followers are found mostly in Asia, North Africa, and the Middle East.

jihad word commonly used to mean a Muslim holy war against enemies of Islam. However, it can also mean a struggle for personal or spiritual perfection.

martyr person who willingly suffers death or disability on behalf of a cause

massacre deliberate killing of a large group of people

moderate views on subjects such as religion or politics that are not extreme

mosque Islamic house of worship

mujahideen rebel fighter in an Islamic country, such as the Afghan fighters in the war against the Soviets

Muslim follower of Islam

occupation act of taking over an area by military force and keeping control of that area for a period of time

Qu'ran holy book of Islam. Also known as the Koran.

radical views on subjects such as religion or politics that are extreme

reform change made in order to improve something

refugee person forced to leave his or her country in order to escape war, food shortages, or other disasters

riyal Saudi Arabian form of money

Soviet Union former group of communist republics that had its capital in Moscow. Russia was the largest and most dominant member of the Soviet Union.

Taliban government set up by radical militant Muslims in Afghanistan in the early 1990s

theocracy government in which religious leaders rule in the name of God

Wahhabism very strict branch of Islam founded in the 1700s. It is practiced mostly in Saudi Arabia, but it has spread in recent decades.

warlord military commander with great independence to do as he or she wishes

Notes on Sources

A DAY IN SEPTEMBER (PAGES 6–7)

1. Robert Sullivan, ed., *One Nation: America Remembers September 11* (New York: Time, 2001), 22.

2. Tom Templeton and Tom Lumley, "9/11 in Numbers," *The Guardian*, August 18, 2002.

3. Sullivan, *One Nation*, 25.

4. Sullivan, *One Nation*, 16.

5. Sullivan, *One Nation*, 29.

6. Andrew Buncombe, "Death Toll of US Troops in Iraq Passes September 11," *The Independent*, December 27, 2006.

7. Susan Headden, "Understanding Islam," *U.S. News and World Report*, April 7, 2008, http://www.usnews.com/articles/news/religion/2008/04/07/understanding-islam.html.

GROWING UP BIN LADEN (PAGES 10–15)

1. "Osama bin Laden's Followers Mark His 50th Birthday on the Web," *USA Today*, March 10, 2007, http://www.usatoday.com/news/world/2007-03-10-bin-laden-birthday_N.htm.

2. Lawrence Wright, *The Looming Tower: Al-Qaeda and the Road to 9/11* (New York, Vintage, 2006), 83.

3. Wright, *The Looming Tower*, 82.

4. Wright, *The Looming Tower*, 29–31.

5. Wright, *The Looming Tower*, 29–31.

6. Wright, *The Looming Tower*, 72–74, 99.

7. Wright, *The Looming Tower*, 82.

8. Wright, *The Looming Tower*, 83–84.

9. Wright, *The Looming Tower*, 83–84; Steve Coll, *The Bin Ladens: An Arabian Family in the American Century* (New York: Penguin, 2008), 37–39.

10. Coll, *The Bin Ladens*, 38.

11. Wright, *The Looming Tower*, 86; Peter L. Bergen, *The Osama bin Laden I Know: An Oral History of al Qaeda's Leader* (New York: Free Press, 2006), 14.

12. Carmen bin Laden, *Inside the Kingdom: My Life in Saudi Arabia* (New York: Warner, 2004), 39.

13. Coll, *The Bin Ladens*, 199.

14. Coll, *The Bin Ladens*, 24, 41.

15. Coll, *The Bin Ladens*, 87.

16. Wright, *The Looming Tower*, 84.

RELIGIOUS AWAKENING (PAGES 18–23)

1. Coll, *The Bin Ladens*, 143.
2. Coll, *The Bin Ladens*, 146.
3. Bin Laden, *Inside the Kingdom*, 162–63; Wright, *The Looming Tower*, 99–100; interview with Mai Yamani et al., *Frontline*, PBS, http://www.pbs.org/wgbh/pages/frontline/shows/saudi/analyses/wahhabism.html; Globalsecurity.org, "Wahhabi," http://www.globalsecurity.org/military/world/gulf/wahhabi.htm.
4. Wright, *The Looming Tower*, 87; Coll, *The Bin Ladens*, 44–46; Bergen, *The Osama bin Laden I Know*, 15.
5. Wright, *The Looming Tower*, 88.
6. Bergen, *The Osama bin Laden I Know*, 14.
7. Wright, *The Looming Tower*, 89.
8. Wright, *The Looming Tower*, 90–92; bin Laden, *Inside the Kingdom*, 161.
9. Bin Laden, *Inside the Kingdom*, 67, 85.
10. Wright, *The Looming Tower*, 92.
11. Wright, *The Looming Tower*, 90.
12. Coll, *The Bin Ladens*, 99; Wright, *The Looming Tower*, 95 ("I want to be"); Bergen, *The Osama bin Laden I Know*, 17, 22.
13. Coll, *The Bin Ladens*, 205–6; Nina Shea, "This Is a Saudi Textbook (After the Intolerance Was Removed)," *The Washington Post*, May 21, 2006.
14. Bergen, *The Osama bin Laden I Know*, 7 ("wanted to get on buses"); Wright, *The Looming Tower*, 45; Coll, *The Bin Ladens*, 204–5.

A YEAR OF RADICAL CHANGE (PAGES 26–31)

1. Bergen, *The Osama bin Laden I Know*, 23.
2. "1979: Shah of Iran Flees into Exile," *BBC News*, http://news.bbc.co.uk/onthisday/hi/dates/stories/january/16/newsid_2530000/2530475.stm.
3. Bin Laden, *Inside the Kingdom*, 117–28.
4. Bin Laden, *Inside the Kingdom*, 117–28.
5. Sandra Mackey, *The Saudis: Inside the Desert Kingdom* (New York: W.W. Norton, 2002), 11.
6. Bin Laden, *Inside the Kingdom*, 120.
7. Bin Laden, *Inside the Kingdom*, 118.
8. Wright, *The Looming Tower*, 101–6.
9. Wright, *The Looming Tower*, 101–6.
10. Wright, *The Looming Tower*, 101–6.
11. Wright, *The Looming Tower*, 101–6.
12. Wright, *The Looming Tower*, 106–8.
13. Bin Laden, *Inside the Kingdom*, 126.

14. Wright, *The Looming Tower*, 109.

15. Wright, *The Looming Tower*, 142–43.

16. Wright, *The Looming Tower*, 142–43.

17. Wright, *The Looming Tower*, 91; *The 9/11 Report: The National Commission on Terrorist Attacks upon the United States* (New York: St. Martin's Press, 2004), 51.

18. Wright, *The Looming Tower*, 91–92; *The 9/11 Report,* 51; Daniel Benjamin and Steven Simon, *The Age of Sacred Terror* (New York: Random House, 2002), 65; Bruce Livesey, "The Salafist Movement," *Frontline*, PBS, http://www.pbs.org/wgbh/pages/frontline/shows/front/special/sala.html.

THE MUJAHIDEEN (PAGES 34–41)

1. Coll, *The Bin Ladens*, 229.

2. Wright, *The Looming Tower*, 94.

3. Wright, *The Looming Tower*, 115; Bergen, *The Osama bin Laden I Know*, 23–24, 49–50.

4. Coll, *The Bin Ladens*, 251–53.

5. Wright, *The Looming Tower*, 109.

6. Brian Handwerk, "What Does 'Jihad' Really Mean to Muslims?" *National Geographic News*, October 24, 2003, http://news.nationalgeographic.com/news/2003/10/1023_031023_jihad.html.

7. Coll, *The Bin Ladens*, 251–52.

8. Wright, *The Looming Tower*, 113–16.

9. Wright, *The Looming Tower*, 116.

10. Wright, *The Looming Tower*, 110.

11. Wright, *The Looming Tower*, 111.

12. Wright, *The Looming Tower*, 111.

13. Wright, *The Looming Tower*, 117–19.

14. Wright, *The Looming Tower*, 123–24.

15. Wright, *The Looming Tower*, 115.

16. Coll, *The Bin Ladens*, 302; Wright, *The Looming Tower*, 31.

17. Coll, *The Bin Ladens*, 302–3.

18. Wright, *The Looming Tower*, 157.

19. Coll, *The Bin Ladens*, 292.

20. Bergen, *The Osama bin Laden I Know*, 60–61.

21. Bergen, *The Osama bin Laden I Know*, 39, 60–61; Coll, *The Bin Ladens*, 292–94.

22. Ahmed Rashid, *Taliban: Militant Islam, Oil and Fundamentalism in Central Asia* (New Haven, CT: Yale Nota Bene, 2001), 129.

23. Bergen, *The Osama bin Laden I Know*, 117, 433; Wright, *The Looming Tower*, 206, 215.

24. Bergen, *The Osama bin Laden I Know*, 117, 433.

FROM HERO TO OUTCAST (PAGES 44–51)

1. Wright, *The Looming Tower*, 151, 167.
2. Coll, *The Bin Ladens*, 336.
3. Wright, *The Looming Tower*, 149.
4. Coll, *The Bin Ladens*, 337–38; Wright, *The Looming Tower*, 152.
5. Wright, *The Looming Tower*, 162.
6. Coll, *The Bin Ladens*, 340–41; Bergen, *The Osama bin Laden I Know*, 92–93.
7. Bergen, *The Osama bin Laden I Know*, 106–7; Wright, *The Looming Tower*, 185.
8. Wright, *The Looming Tower*, 187.
9. Bergen, *The Osama bin Laden I Know*, 110.
10. Wright, *The Looming Tower*, 174.
11. Wright, *The Looming Tower*, 174–76.
12. Wright, *The Looming Tower*, 176–78.
13. Wright, *The Looming Tower*, 179.
14. Bergen, *The Osama bin Laden I Know*, 168.
15. Bergen, *The Osama bin Laden I Know*, 181.
16. Bergen, *The Osama bin Laden I Know*, 172.

AL QAEDA DECLARES WAR (PAGES 54–63)

1. Wright, *The Looming Tower*, 182–83.
2. Wright, *The Looming Tower*, 187.
3. Wright, *The Looming Tower*, 191–92.
4. Wright, *The Looming Tower*, 191.
5. Wright, *The Looming Tower*, 253.
6. Wright, *The Looming Tower*, 190–92.
7. Wright, *The Looming Tower*, 194–95.
8. Wright, *The Looming Tower*, 189.
9. Wright, *The Looming Tower*, 197.
10. Bergen, *The Osama bin Laden I Know*, 116.
11. Wright, *The Looming Tower*, 215–17.
12. Bergen, *The Osama bin Laden I Know*, 137–39; Wright, *The Looming Tower*, 193, 214.
13. Wright, *The Looming Tower*, 198.
14. Bergen, *The Osama bin Laden I Know*, 200–203.
15. Wright, *The Looming Tower*, 203.
16. Wright, *The Looming Tower*, 348.

17. Wright, *The Looming Tower*, 217–18.

18. Bergen, *The Osama bin Laden I Know*, 164–66.

19. Wright, *The Looming Tower*, 218–20.

20. Bergen, *The Osama bin Laden I Know*, 151–52; Wright, *The Looming Tower*, 222.

21. Wright, *The Looming Tower*, 249–52.

22. Wright, *The Looming Tower*, 223, 226.

AL QAEDA STRIKES (PAGES 66–73)

1. Wright, *The Looming Tower*, 256.

2. Wright, *The Looming Tower*, 261–62.

3. Wright, *The Looming Tower*, 260.

4. Wright, *The Looming Tower*, 281.

5. Wright, *The Looming Tower*, 286.

6. Wright, *The Looming Tower*, 284.

7. Bergen, *The Osama bin Laden I Know*, 182; Wright, *The Looming Tower*, 279–80.

8. Bergen, *The Osama bin Laden I Know*, 183–84; Wright, *The Looming Tower*, 279.

9. Wright, *The Looming Tower*, 295.

10. Wright, *The Looming Tower*, 306–7.

11. Wright, *The Looming Tower*, 306–8.

12. Wright, *The Looming Tower*, 312–17; *The 9/11 Report*, 169.

13. Wright, *The Looming Tower*, 319–20.

14. Wright, *The Looming Tower*, 323.

15. Bergen, *The Osama bin Laden I Know*, 231; Wright, *The Looming Tower*, 323–24.

16. Bergen, *The Osama bin Laden I Know*, 396; Wright, *The Looming Tower*, 326.

17. Wright, *The Looming Tower*, 337, 341.

18. Bergen, *The Osama bin Laden I Know*, 438; Wright, *The Looming Tower*, 338.

19. Bergen, *The Osama bin Laden I Know*, 251; Wright, *The Looming Tower*, 361.

20. Wright, *The Looming Tower*, 374–75.

21. Bernard Haykel, "Osama bin Laden: The Islamic Bard of Terror," *Japan Times*, July 23, 2008; Wright, *The Looming Tower*, 376–77; Bergen, *The Osama bin Laden I Know*, 254–56.

SEPTEMBER 11 (PAGES 76–83)

1. Terry McDermott, *Perfect Soldiers: The Hijackers: Who They Were, Why They Did It* (New York: HarperCollins, 2005), xiii.

2. McDermott, *Perfect Soldiers*, 228; Sullivan, *One Nation*, 20–29.

3. Jane Corbin, *Al-Qaeda: In Search of the Terror Network That Threatens the World* (New York: Thunder's Mouth Press, 2002), 218.

4. McDermott, *Perfect Soldiers*, 250; Bergen, *The Osama bin Laden I Know*, 194; "Research Reveals New Profile of Suicide Bombers," *Morning Edition*, NPR, March 7, 2003, http://www.npr.org/programs/morning/transcripts/2003/mar/030307.joyce.html.

5. Bergen, *The Osama bin Laden I Know*, 255; Wright, *The Looming Tower*, 375.

6. Wright, *The Looming Tower*, 382.

7. Wright, *The Looming Tower*, 5–7, 321, 350–51, 381, 384, 388.

8. Bergen, *The Osama bin Laden I Know*, 418.

9. Bergen, *The Osama bin Laden I Know*, 420–21.

10. McDermott, *Perfect Soldiers*, 227; Wright, *The Looming Tower*, 384.

11. Wright, *The Looming Tower*, 389.

12. Wright, *The Looming Tower*, 378–79.

13. Wright, *The Looming Tower*, 401.

14. Sullivan, *One Nation*, 20–29.

15. Sullivan, *One Nation*, 20–29.

16. *The 9/11 Report*, 468; History.com, "Grounding of Planes on 11th September 2001," http://www.history.com/content/9-11/grounding-of-planes-on-11th-sept.

17. Author's personal experience.

18. Andrew Buncombe, "Death Toll."

19. Nationmaster.com, "Terrorism Statistics: Victims of the September 11th 2001 Attacks (most recent) by Country," http://www.nationmaster.com/graph/ter_vic_of_the_sep_11t_200_att-victims-september-11th-2001-attacks.

20. Eric Lipton, "A Nation Challenged: The Toll: In Cold Numbers, a Census of the Sept. 11 Victims," *New York Times*, April 19, 2002.

21. National Institute of Mental Health, "Post-Traumatic Stress Disorder," http://www.nimh.nih.gov/health/publications/post-traumatic-stress-disorder-a-real-illness/summary.shtml.

22. Templeton and Lumley, "9/11 in Numbers."

CATCHING BIN LADEN (PAGES 86–93)

1. Bergen, *The Osama bin Laden I Know*, 315.

2. Corbin, *Al-Qaeda*, 245.

3. Bergen, *The Osama bin Laden I Know*, 317; Corbin, *Al-Qaeda*, 247.

4. Phillip Carter, "Tainted by Torture: How Evidence Obtained Through Coercion Is Undermining the Legal War on Terrorism," *Slate*, May 14, 2004, http:// www.slate.com/id/2100543; Jackie Northam, "Q&A About Guantánamo Bay and the Detainees," NPR, June 23, 2005, http://www.npr.org/templates/story/story.php?storyId=4715916.

5. Corbin, *Al-Qaeda*, 252.

6. Bergen, *The Osama bin Laden I Know*, 321, 331–32.

7. Bergen, *The Osama bin Laden I Know*, 320.

8. Bergen, *The Osama bin Laden I Know*, 371.

9. Bergen, *The Osama bin Laden I Know*, 318; Coll, *The Bin Ladens*, 574.

10. "U.S. Pulls Out of Saudi Arabia," BBC News, April 29, 2003, http://news.bbc.co.uk/2/hi/middle_east/2984547.stm; Bergen, *The Osama bin Laden I Know*, 391.

11. Bergen, *The Osama bin Laden I Know*, 371.

12. Bergen, *The Osama bin Laden I Know*, 392.

13. Alastair Leithead, "Taleban at Kabul's Doorstep," *BBC News*, August 13, 2008, http://news.bbc.co.uk/2/hi/south_asia/7555996.stm.

14. Pew Global Attitudes Project, "The Great Divide: How Westerners and Muslims View Each Other," June 22, 2006, http://pewglobal.org/reports/display.php?ReportID=253.

15. "Bin Laden Admits 9/11 Responsibility, Warns of More Attacks," *Online News Hour*, PBS, October 29, 2004, http://www.pbs.org/newshour/updates/binladen_10-29-04.html.

16. Bergen, *The Osama bin Laden I Know*, 317, 321; Wright, *The Looming Tower*, 409–13.

17. Bergen, *The Osama bin Laden I Know*, 391.

18. Pew Global Attitudes Project.

19. Bergen, *The Osama bin Laden I Know*, 391.

20. Bergen, *The Osama bin Laden I Know*, 391–93.

21. Coll, *The Bin Ladens*, 573.

22. Coll, *The Bin Ladens*, 533.

Further Reading

Bergen, Peter L., *The Osama bin Laden I Know: An Oral History of al Qaeda's Leader*. New York: Free Press, 2006

Berntsen, Gary and Pezzullo, Ralph. *Jawbreaker: The Attack on Bin Laden and Al Qaeda: A Personal Account by the CIA's Key Field Commander.* New York: Crown, 2005

Bin Laden, Carmen. I*nside the Kingdom: My Life in Saudi Arabia*, New York: Warner, 2004

Bin Laden, Osama. *Messages to the World: The Statements of Osama bin Laden*, New York: Verso, 2005

Coll, Steve, *The Bin Ladens: An Arabian Family in the American Century*. New York: The Penguin Press, 2008

Coll, Steve. *Ghost Wars: The Secret History of the CIA, Afghanistan, and bin Laden, from the Soviet Invasion to September 10, 2001*. New York: Penguin, 2004

Corbin, Jane, *Al-Qaeda: In Search of the Terror Network that Threatens the World*. New York: Thunder's Mouth Press, 2002

Ibrahim, Raymond. *The Al Qaeda Reader*. New York: Broadway, 2007

Leeming, Matthew and Omrani, Bijan. *Afghanistan: A Companion and Guide*. New York: Odyssey, 2005

Mackey, Sandra. *The Saudis: Inside the Desert Kingdom*. New York: Norton, 2002

McDermott, Terry, *Perfect Soldiers: The Hijackers: Who They Were, Why They Did It*. New York: HarperCollins, 2005

Rashid, Ahmed. *Descent into Chaos: The U.S. and the Disaster in Pakistan, Afghanistan, and Central Asia*. New York: Penguin, 2009

Rashid, Ahmed. *Taliban: Militant Islam, Oil and Fundamentalism in Central Asia*, New Haven, Conn.: Yale Nota Bene, 2001

Sullivan, Robert, ed., *One Nation: America Remembers September 11*. New York: Time, 2001

Tanner, Steven. *Afghanistan: A Military History from Alexander the Great to the War against the Taliban*. New York: Da Capo Press, 2009

Trofimov, Yaroslav. *The Siege of Mecca: The 1979 Uprising at Islam's Holiest Shrine*. New York: Anchor, 2008

Wright, Lawrence, *The Looming Tower: Al-Qaeda and the Road to 9/11*. New York: Vintage, 2006

The 9/11 Report: The National Commission on Terrorist Attacks Upon the United States, New York: St. Martin's Press, 2004

Find Out More

Tracking bin Laden
http://www.pbs.org/wgbh/pages/frontline/shows/binladen/

This companion website to the PBS documentary "Hunting Bin Laden" shows viewers the difficulties that U.S. forces face in trying to track down the world's most wanted terrorist and his organization.

Al Qaeda's Message
http://www.pbs.org/wgbh/pages/frontline/shows/front/

This companion website to the PBS documentary "Al Qaeda's New Front" shows the efforts al Qaeda has made since September 11, 2001, to bring its message of radical Islam to the Middle East.

Bin Laden Article
http://news.bbc.co.uk/2/hi/south_asia/155236.stm

This BBC News profile of Osama bin Laden contains links to footage of him and stories about his activities. It provides good first-hand looks at Osama in action.

Fighting Terrorism
http://news.bbc.co.uk/2/hi/in_depth/world/2001/war_on_terror/default.stm

This BBC website helps explain the efforts made to combat terrorism. It includes a who's who of terrorists as well as explanations of various controversies, such as the U.S. detention of terror suspects in Cuba.

A Wanted Man
http://www.fbi.gov/wanted/topten/fugitives/laden.htm

This website shows a copy of the FBI's wanted poster on bin Laden.

Most-Wanted Terrorists
http://www.fbi.gov/wanted/terrorists/fugitives.htm

This FBI website shows the current list of "most wanted" terrorist fugitives. It provides details about their backgrounds and explains why they are being hunted by law enforcement.

Bin Laden's Youth
http://www.newyorker.com/archive/2005/12/12/051212fa_fact

This New Yorker article gives insight into bin Laden's younger years and explains how those early influences led him to become a Muslim extremist. The article quotes former teachers and fellow classmates about what Bin Laden was like and how he changed over time.

9/11 Biographies

http://www.nytimes.com/pages/national/portraits/

The New York Times *compiled brief biographies of all the September 11 victims. These biographies show the incredible variety among the nearly 3,000 people who died that day. They also personalize the tragedy as few other sources can.*

The Global Impact of 9/11

www.nationmaster.com/graph/ter_vic_of_the_sep_11t_200_att-victims-september-11th-2001-attacks

This website uses basic statistics to show the wide range of nationalities represented among the September 11 victims. Many people probably do not realize that countries like Japan and Colombia lost large numbers of citizens that day.

Muslim Views

http://pewglobal.org/reports/display.php?ReportID=253

This Pew Global Attitudes Project report breaks down attitudes toward bin Laden in the Muslim world. This report shows the wide range of opinions found in the Muslim world and shows how those opinions change based on geography.

Conspiracy Theories

http://www.popularmechanics.com/technology/military_law/1227842.html

Like many famous events, the September 11 attacks have become the subject of wild conspiracy theories. This Popular Mechanics website debunks many myths and explains many of the strange-but-true events of that day.

The 9/11 Commission

http://www.9-11commission.gov/report/index.htm

This is the official website of the 9/11 Commission. The commission investigated the attacks for the U.S. government and issued a report explaining what happened and what the government needs to do to help prevent future terrorist attacks.

9/11 Retrospective

http://www.time.com/time/covers/1101020909/index.html

Time *magazine produced this website commemorating the September 11 attacks. The site's retrospective helps put the attack in context and explains what has happened since that terrible day.*

The CIA on Terrorism

https://www.cia.gov/news-information/cia-the-war-on-terrorism/index.html

This CIA website on combating al Qaeda includes a FAQ on terrorism. It also provides valuable resources such as a manual on weapons of mass destruction and links to anti-terror websites such as the Department of Homeland Security.

Index